Vincent van Gogh

Portrait of an Artist

Jan Greenberg and Sandra Jordan

DELACORTE PRESS

Published by
Delacorte Press
an imprint of
Random House Children's Books
a division of Random House, Inc.
1540 Broadway
New York, New York 10036

Visit us on the Web! www.randomhouse.com/kids
Educators and librarians, for a variety of teaching tools, visit us at
www.randomhouse.com/teachers

Library of Congress Cataloging-in-Publication Data

Greenberg, Jan.
    Vincent van Gogh : portrait of an artist / Jan Greenberg and Sandra Jordan.
        p. cm.
    Includes bibliographical references.
    ISBN 0-385-32806-0 (trade) — ISBN 0-385-90005-8 (lib.bdg.)
    1. Gogh, Vincent van, 1853–1890—Juvenile literature.
    2. Painters—Netherlands—Biography—Juvenile literature.
    [1. Gogh, Vincent van, 1853–1890. 2. Artists.] I. Jordan, Sandra. II. Title.

ND653.G7 V535 2001
759.9492—dc21
                                                                00-031850

The text of this book is set in 12-point Goudy.

Book design by Patrice Sheridan

Manufactured in the United States of America

August 2001

10 9 8 7 6 5 4 3 2 1

BVG

Vincent van Gogh

Portrait of an Artist

For Benjamin, Lilly, and Alexander.
J.G.

For Kathryn Bondi. Miss you.
S.J.

With special thanks to Cornelia Homburg,
Assistant Director for Curatorial Affairs
at the Saint Louis Art Museum

Contents

viii   Contents

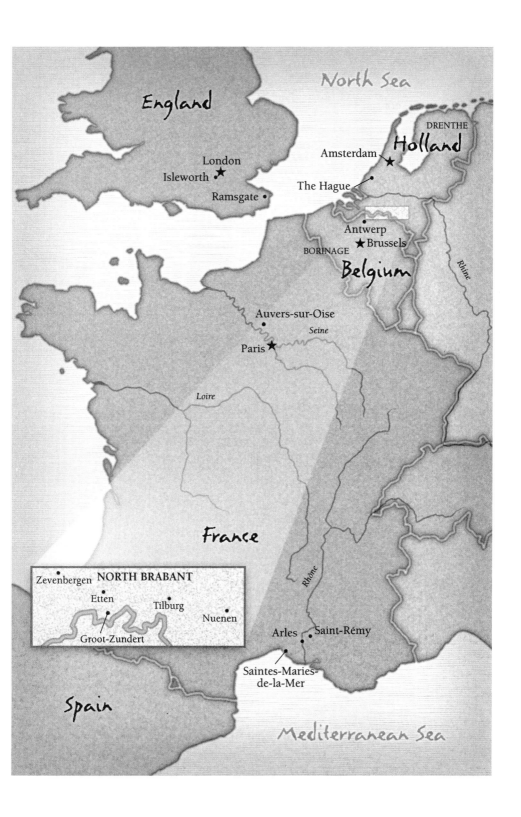

Prologue

HUNCHED LIKE A PORCUPINE from the weight of his easel, brushes, tubes of color, and folding stool, Vincent headed out of Arles at dawn—too early for the gang of street boys to chase after him, to call him crazy. In the pocket of his workman's smock he carried lunch, a piece of bread and a bottle of milk. That was all he needed. He would catch the sun as it poured its first light on the glistening wheat fields.

In front of him lay the wide plain called the Crau, laden with ripe grain. It reminded him of the flat landscape of Holland, where he grew up—land that stretched out to the horizon, as beautiful and infinite as the sea. But instead of the soft, clear northern light, the fierce Provençal sun cascaded bright yellow rays on the rooftops, trees, and fields. Everywhere he looked shimmered old gold, bronze, and copper against the greenish azure of the sky.

Vincent braced the legs of his easel with rocks to steady it against the strong winds that blew down the valley. He squeezed paint onto his palette: emerald green, Prussian blue,

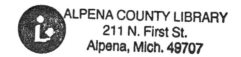

crimson lake, chrome yellow, cobalt violet, orange lead. The mental labor of balancing the six essential colors strained his mind, as though he were a stage actor playing multiple parts.

He brought out his largest canvas, a size thirty, twenty-nine inches by thirty-six inches. Early in his career a blank white canvas had challenged him to fill it, mocked his limitations, dared him to bring it to life. Now he didn't hesitate. He picked up his brush and began to paint.

The rhythmic hiss of the farmers' scythes through the grain matched his strokes. Dust from the cut wheat filled the air. Spanish flies, gold and green, swarmed around the olive trees. The grasshopper-like cicadas sang in the field, as loud as frogs. Mosquitoes buzzed and bit. Vincent painted on.

In the foreground of the canvas, a fence sheltered fruit trees from the wind. Across the middle stretched flat rectangles of fields colored citron, yellow, tan, and ochre; a towering haystack balanced the white farmhouses with their red tile roofs. Harvesters bundled the cut grain, stacked the wheat, handed it up into the high window of the mill. A man drove a cart. Each person went intently about a task as Vincent drew them with a few strokes of his brush. In the distance stood the pale violet of the hills and the ruined abbey of Montmajour. Overhead spread the blue-green sky, bleached pale by the bright, shadowless light. And in the center of the painting, cool and unobtrusive in all the vibrant yellowness of the scene, sat an empty blue farm cart, its spoked wheel the hub around which the painting revolved.

Vincent had drawn several preliminary studies, preparing for this moment. Now he worked quickly, with feverish energy, to finish the painting in a day. Later, in the studio, he might touch up a few details, but here existed the feeling he wanted to portray. Drenched with sweat, he labored as intently as the harvesters he painted. And standing before *Harvest at Le Crau*, palette and brush in his hand, he lost all sense of time and space. He hardly noticed the heat or his thirst. As the light faded he studied the canvas. His eyes, though bloodshot and tired, did not deceive. A masterpiece, at last! A painting his brother Theo would be proud to show in Paris! After years of struggle he had captured what he called "the high yellow note," vivid color and emotion in perfect harmony. To reach it, he had pushed himself over the edge. But, for now, all that mattered was the intoxication of this moment.

A Brabant Boy
1853 – 75

I have nature and art and poetry. If that is not enough what is?
—LETTER TO THEO, JANUARY 1874

ON MARCH 30, 1853, the handsome, soberly dressed Reverend Theodorus van Gogh entered the ancient town hall of Groot-Zundert, in the Brabant, a province of the Netherlands. He opened the birth register to number twenty-nine, where exactly one year earlier he sadly had written "Vincent Willem van Gogh, stillborn." Beside the inscription he wrote again "Vincent Willem van Gogh," the name of his new, healthy son, who was sleeping soundly next to his mother in the tiny parsonage across the square. The baby's arrival was an answered prayer for the still-grieving family.

The first Vincent lay buried in a tiny grave by the door of the church where Pastor van Gogh preached. The Vincent who lived grew to be a sturdy redheaded boy. Every Sunday on his way to church, young Vincent would pass the headstone carved with the name he shared. Did he feel as if his dead brother were the rightful Vincent, the one who would remain perfect in his parents' hearts, and that he was merely an unsatisfactory replacement? That might have been one of the reasons he spent so much of his life feeling like a lonely outsider, as if he didn't fit anywhere in the world.

Despite his dramatic beginning, Vincent had an ordinary childhood, giving no hint of the painter he would become. The small parsonage, with an upstairs just two windows wide under a slanting roof, quickly grew crowded. By the time he was six he had two sisters, Anna and Elizabeth, and one brother, Theo, whose gentle nature made him their mother's favorite. The youngest van Goghs, Wilhelmien (called Wil) and Cornelius, were born after Vincent went away to school.

Their mother, Anna Carbentus van Gogh, herself one of eight, came from an artistic background. Her father had been a bookbinder to the royal family. A gifted amateur artist who filled notebooks with drawings of plants and flowers, she thought Vincent had a pleasant talent that might be useful someday. She didn't suspect he would develop into a great artist. In fact she recalled only that he once modeled an elephant out of clay but smashed it when she and his father praised it more than he thought they should. For the same reason he tore up a drawing of a cat climbing a tree. It wasn't his artistic ability but his obstinate personality that left the biggest impression on his mother. That willful stubbornness turned up again and again as he grew older.

With a big family and a little house, the children spent a lot of time out of doors. The freckled, red-haired Vincent, solitary by nature, often wandered by himself in the fields and heaths that surrounded the parsonage. He became familiar with the

seasons of planting and harvest and with the hardworking local farm families whose labors connected them to the soil.
The strong feeling he developed for the rural landscape of
Brabant and the lives of its peasants would be one of the major influences in his life.

Mostly he did what boys like to do. He collected bugs and
birds' nests. He teased his sisters. He built sand castles in the garden with Theo. Sometimes he invented games for all of them to
play. After one exciting day his brothers and sisters thanked
Vincent by staging a ceremony, and, with mock formality, pre-
sented him with a rosebush from their father's garden.

Theodorus, Vincent's father, a pastor from a long line of
pastors, was one of eleven children. His family had been members of the bourgeois for generations, with middle-class connections all over the Netherlands. People in Groot-Zundert
called Mr. van Gogh the "Handsome Pastor" for his good
looks but found his long sermons boring. The province of Brabant, where the village was located, was a farming district
populated mainly by Catholics. The pastor's Dutch Reformed
congregation had only 120 members, and as a result, he didn't
make much money. Family finances were tight. Vincent attended the village school until his parents, worried that the
peasant children were making their son rough, hired a gov-
erness to teach the children at home.

When Vincent was only eleven, his parents sent him away
to Mr. Provily's school in the nearby town of Zevenbergen.
Waving goodbye on the steps of the school, he watched his
mother and father's little yellow carriage drive down the road
until it disappeared. The gray autumn sky matched his mood.
His parents noticed how sad he looked. A few weeks later, as
Vincent stood in the corner of the playground, someone told

him he had a visitor. His father had come back to check on him. Overcome with emotion, Vincent fell on his father's neck, but still he had to remain in school. Though he would visit and even live at home in the years to follow, it was the beginning of what he felt to be a life of exile.

Vincent's schoolmasters didn't consider him an outstanding student. He was intelligent but no scholar. Still, after two years at Mr. Provily's, Vincent moved up. His parents valued education, and they sent their eldest son to an impressive new school in the nearby town of Tilburg—King Willem II State Secondary School.

The school had nine teachers for only thirty-six pupils, so Vincent's days were busy. He took a long list of courses: Dutch, German, French, English, arithmetic, history, geography, geometry, botany, zoology, gymnastics, calligraphy, linear drawing, and freehand drawing. The drawing classes were considered part of a well-rounded gentleman's education, not preparation for a career. He ended his first term well enough to be one of five boys in his class of ten who were promoted. However, in March of the following year, the family took him out of school, probably for financial reasons. He left with a passion for novels and poetry and a working knowledge of four languages. In that era many children finished school at fifteen and apprenticed in a trade, but Vincent sat at home for more than a year before the family reached a decision about his future.

Three of his father's five brothers—Uncle Vincent (whose nickname was Cent), Uncle Cor, and Uncle Heim—owned flourishing art galleries, the charismatic Uncle Cent being the most successful of the three. The French firm of Goupil et Cie, with headquarters in Paris and branches in London, Brussels, and The Hague, had purchased his gallery and made him a partner. Cent, now semiretired for health reasons, maintained an interest in the firm. Married but with no children of his own, he took an active role in the lives of his young nephews and nieces. So Vincent, his namesake, was offered an opportunity to learn the art business.

In July 1869 Vincent began his apprenticeship in The Hague, an elegant and historic town that was the center of the Netherlands government. The Goupil gallery branch there looked like an upper-class drawing room, not a commercial establishment. Doorways between the rooms were draped with swags of heavy fabric trimmed with fringe. Oriental rugs covered the floors. On the brocaded walls, gold-framed pictures hung all the way to the ceiling. Customers at Goupil could see for themselves how the paintings would look in their own richly decorated houses.

The town might have seemed overwhelming to a sixteen-year-old fresh from the countryside, but Vincent's mother had grown up in The Hague and still had many connections there. Vincent boarded with cousins who could be counted on to look after him. He enthusiastically set about learning his new trade and spent his free hours looking at art, rather than socializing. In nearby Amsterdam, only thirty-three miles away, he visited his uncle Cor's gallery and happily spent hours in Amsterdam's old art museum, whose crowded walls glowed with the great Dutch and Flemish painters of the past, including Rembrandt, Vermeer, and Hals.

In August 1872, after he had been in The Hague for three years, his brother Theo, still a schoolboy, came to see him. The two boys went sight-seeing one afternoon, walking to a mill on the outskirts of town. There they took shelter from a sudden rainstorm and talked of their dreams for the future. Over a pitcher of milk, the brothers vowed eternal friendship, an extraordinary bond that lasted the rest of their lives. A few days later Vincent wrote to thank Theo for coming, and sympathized with his long trek to school in the August heat. This simple note began a correspondence of more than six hundred letters, in which Vincent chronicled almost every aspect of his life and art.

Four years after Vincent joined Goupil, Theo also apprenticed at the firm, starting in the branch in Brussels, Belgium, since the company's managers didn't want two brothers in the same office. Vincent regretted that they couldn't work together, but he didn't have long to grieve about it. Goupil transferred him to the London office to learn the English part of the business. The promotion marked the firm's confidence in Vincent's future. He had done well in The Hague, and the director, Mr. Tersteeg, wrote to his parents that clients as well as painters enjoyed dealing with their son, and that he was certain Vincent would be a success in his profession.

In 1873 Queen Victoria sat on the throne of an England that was undergoing a tumultuous shift from a rural farming economy to an urban manufacturing one. The prosperous city of London bustled with contagious energy. Vincent celebrated his promotion by purchasing a new top hat and a pair of gloves. Such items of clothing, he solemnly assured his parents, were necessary in England. In his first enthusiastic rush, he approved of almost everything he saw—the flowers, the people riding their horses in the park, the poor children playing in the streets.

He rented a room a brisk forty-five-minute walk from the Goupil offices and happily settled in. His lodgings had "a room such as I always longed for, without a slanting ceiling and without blue paper." The landlady of this suburban boardinghouse was a clergyman's widow, Ursula Loyer. Vincent, alone in a strange country for the first time, found her warm, motherly manner attractive. Even more appealing to him was Ursula's nineteen-year-old daughter, Eugénie. A slim, dark-haired girl with charming manners, Eugénie Loyer helped with the boarders and ran a small nursery school on the property.

When Vincent met Eugénie she was secretly engaged to one of their former boarders, the man she ultimately married. She might have flirted with Vincent, but she never seriously considered him as a suitor. Unfortunately, it didn't take much to captivate his lonely heart. The shy twenty-year-old with a thick Dutch accent had almost no experience with women.

Vincent's infatuation with Eugénie was apparent to his sister Anna, who had moved to London and lived with Vincent at the Loyers' while looking for a teaching job. Vincent claimed he regarded Eugénie as another sister, but Anna told the family her brother was in love, whether or not he admitted it. He apparently proposed several times, and when he couldn't change Eugénie's mind, the two van Goghs moved to a new place. Instead of confiding in Theo, Vincent stopped writing for almost six months, one of only three major breaks in their correspondence.

His family believed him brokenhearted, blaming that for the dramatic change in his work and personality. The cheerful Vincent who had written to a friend that he was happy "having nothing, yet possessing all" turned silent, moody, and difficult. He refused to go out, preferring his own company. For the first time people called him eccentric, a word often used to describe him as time passed.

In 1875, hoping that a change of scene would improve his

outlook, Goupil transferred Vincent again, this time to one of their Paris offices. Uncle Cent assumed that a single man of twenty-two would find the lively capital of France a perfect place to leave his disappointing love affair behind. Vincent appreciated the museums and galleries, particularly the Louvre and the Luxembourg Palace, but life in Paris held no special charm for him. Instead of sampling the Parisian nightlife, he began attending church regularly for the first time since he had left home.

At some point Vincent may have fallen under the spell of one of the evangelistic preachers he went to hear on Sundays. He and his roommate, a fellow worker at Goupil, spent all their free time reading the Bible. Vincent's letters to Theo and his parents brimmed with mention of texts, hymns, and sermons he had attended. He even advised his brother to destroy all his books except the Bible. This, too, was new from Vincent, who always had written fervently about paintings, novels, and scenery, but not about religion. To his alarmed family, his behavior bordered on the fanatic.

At Christmastime Vincent couldn't wait to go home. A crisis loomed, and he needed to consult his father. Despite caring deeply about art, he could no longer tolerate the art business. He spoke rudely to customers, challenging their taste and criticizing their purchases. His employer discouraged him from taking time off—the holidays were the busiest sales time in the Paris offices—but Vincent could be recklessly persistent. His father had a new parish in Etten, yet another small town in Brabant, and to Etten he went.

When he returned after Christmas, Vincent commented to his boss, Mr. Boussod, the head of the Paris branches of Goupil, that he trusted there were no complaints about his work. If he had not initiated the conversation, Mr. Boussod would have. As Vincent said, "When the apple is ripe, a soft breeze makes it fall from the tree." After an unpleasant conversation that touched on Vincent's absence, his unusual choices of clothing, and his tactless handling of clients, Mr. Boussod fired him. Vincent was out of a job.

Vincent in England
1876–77

*How rich art is. If one can only remember what one has seen,
one is never empty of thoughts or truly lonely, never alone.*
—LETTER TO THEO, NOVEMBER 1878

VINCENT, HOMESICK BUT TRYING to make the best of it,
sketched the view looking out the window of a small school in
Ramsgate, England. The scratchy picture—a lamppost, a
curving driveway, the corner of a building, and beyond it the
ocean—was for Theo. "Enclosed is a little drawing of the view
from the school window where the boys wave good-by to their
parents when they are going back to the station after a visit.
No one of us will ever forget the view from the window,"
Vincent wrote.

After many letters and inquiries, he finally had found a
position at a small boarding school for poor English boys
between the ages of ten and fourteen. He received no salary.

Mr. Stokes, who ran the school, said he could attract all the teachers he needed in return for food and lodging.

Although Mr. Stokes played marbles with his students and took them for walks on the beach, Vincent reported that Stokes sometimes lost his temper. "When the boys make more noise than he likes, they occasionally have to go without their supper. I wish you could see them looking from the window then, it is rather melancholy; they have so little else except their meals to look forward to and help them pass their days."

The school resembled something out of Vincent's favorite English author, Charles Dickens. Roaches crawled all over the old building. The room where the boys washed had rotten floorboards and broken windowpanes through which the wind whistled, but the view of the ocean almost compensated for the discomfort. Ramsgate was a charming seaside village of about six thousand people almost eighty miles from London. Vincent's letters describing the area to Theo display an eloquence that his drawings had yet to achieve. "The ground we walk on was all covered with big gray stones, chalk and shells. To the right lay the sea as calm as a pond, reflecting the light of the transparent gray sky where the sun was setting."

Scenic vistas, however, were not enough to sustain him. When Mr. Stokes moved his school from Ramsgate to Isleworth, closer to London, Vincent began to look for other work. He had turned his back on the art business and now announced that "there were no professions in the world other than those of schoolmaster and clergyman, with all that lies between these two—such as missionary, especially a London missionary."

He accepted a new job at a school in Isleworth with the Reverend Mr. Slade-Jones, who at least paid him a meager salary. More exciting was the opportunity Mr. Slade-Jones offered him to preach. Vincent read Bible stories with the boys and taught Bible history. His letters home, crammed with religious meditations, caused his parents to worry about his lack of balance. If their son wanted to be an evangelist, his father fretted, he should start the necessary studies, not go on and on in this unpractical way.

In October 1876 Vincent preached his first real sermon: "Sorrow is better than joy—and even in mirth the heart is sad—and it is better to go to the house of mourning than to the house of feasts, for by the sadness of the countenance the heart is made better." It wasn't a crowd pleaser. The gloomy message aside, he was not a good speaker. Like his father, he lacked the gift of inspiring his listeners, and certainly his heavy accent didn't help.

Even without preaching, the schedule at Mr. Slade-Jones's school was grueling, and Vincent labored nonstop. He taught languages, lectured on the Bible, weeded the garden, tutored, and acted as the school's bill collector. Exhausted, he returned home for the Christmas holidays. His younger sister Elizabeth, who looked forward to having fun with him, instead found her brother "groggy with piety." Vincent informed his family that his experience in Isleworth had revealed his true mission in life. Following the van Gogh tradition of his father, grandfather, and great-grandfather, he would become a clergyman.

His family doubted Vincent's chances for success in this vocation. It was clear, however, that for now he was better off in the Netherlands, and Vincent wrote a long letter to Slade-Jones and his wife explaining why he wouldn't be coming back.

Uncle Cent found him a temporary job working in a bookstore, where Vincent spent most of his time in the back room, polishing his language skills by translating the Bible from

Dutch into English, French, and German. At the boarding-house where he stayed, his roommate reported that Vincent lived like a saint, refusing meat and existing on a Spartan diet of bread and boiled vegetables. His only luxury was a little to-bacco for the pipe he had started smoking, and on at least one occasion he gave that up to buy food for a hungry stray dog. On Sundays Vincent amused himself by attending services at four or five different churches. He had made up his mind about his calling. Unfortunately, it took more than desire to be a pastor.

For ordination in the Dutch Reformed Church, he would need to pass state entrance examinations, then train for six expensive years at the theological seminary in Amsterdam. Vincent spoke four languages but not the required Greek and Latin. He knew a great deal about art and literature, but didn't have a high-school degree. Preparing for the exams might take as much as two years of tutoring.

His parents suspected that at age twenty-four their son was unlikely to develop academic discipline, but without a degree, they knew, he wouldn't be eligible for a meaningful job in the church. The whole extended family organized themselves to help Vincent out—all except Uncle Cent, who called Vin-cent's latest ambition ridiculous. Uncle Jan, the commandant of the naval shipyard in Amsterdam, offered Vincent room and board in his large house. Uncle Cor gave him paper and other supplies. And Uncle Stricker, a successful pastor and published author, supervised his studies and found him tutors.

Uncle Jan's house overlooked the huge shipyard, and Vin-cent delighted in the hustle and bustle of the wharves. He compared the sound of footsteps of three thousand workmen on their way home to the roaring of the sea. He found his studies less enjoyable. All too soon the reality of what he had

undertaken began to worry him. It proved to be "much difficult work which I do not like—which I, or rather my evil self,
would like to shirk."

Vincent began to feel constantly anxious. In his uneasy
dreams solid, well-meaning relatives stared at him reproach-
fully. After all their help, how could he fail them? He tried to
keep his letters to Theo cheerful, filled with news of his studies and visits to family members and their friends, but sometimes the effort was beyond him. He wrote that he had
breakfasted on a piece of dry bread and a glass of beer—that
being the remedy Charles Dickens advised for those who are
on the point of committing suicide.

Mendes da Costa, a young rabbi not much older than Vincent, tutored him in Latin and Greek. Da Costa liked his
freckle-faced student, who might be homely but whose appearance had a "charming quaintness." He was particularly
impressed by Vincent's gentle manner with the da Costa family's aunt. While many people mocked the old woman for her
twisted body and slow wits, Vincent always treated her kindly.
She eagerly hurried to answer the door when he came for his
lessons, and Vincent told da Costa that she was a good soul—
even if she did mispronounce his name.

Perhaps because they were close in age, Vincent confessed
to da Costa what the pressures had driven him to do. For fail-
ures, real or imagined, he punished himself by beating his
back with a rope or else locking himself out of his uncle's
house and sleeping in a cold shed without a blanket.

This extreme behavior did nothing to help his concentra-
tion—or his growing negative feelings toward the whole
academic enterprise. Vincent excelled at languages and didn't
mind Latin, but Greek he found a waste of time. "Mendes,"
he said, "do you seriously believe that such horrors are

indispensable to a man who wants to do what I want to do: give peace to poor creatures and reconcile them to their existence here on earth." After a year of struggling, Vincent asked Mendes to tell his uncle Stricker that it was useless. He would not be able to pass his entrance examinations.

Instead of looking for a profession better suited to his talents, Vincent went to Brussels, Belgium, with his father and his friend Slade-Jones, who traveled from Isleworth to help him. The English clergyman knew of an evangelical course there that took three years instead of six. Vincent was accepted on a trial basis.

If he knew what *trial* meant, it didn't make any impression on him. When asked during a grammar lesson whether a word was in the nominative or the dative case, he replied, "Oh, sir, I really don't care." His father received alarming reports that Vincent starved himself and slept on the floor instead of the bed. He visited his son and tried to put him back on track, but without success. At the end of his trial period Vincent was told he could stay, but not on the same inexpensive terms as the students from Belgium.

Vincent refused to ask his parents to pay for more schooling. He wangled a six-month assignment as an evangelist and once more set out on a journey, this time to the Borinage, a grim mining district in southwestern Belgium, "far from the land of pictures."

The Missionary
1879–80

There may be a great fire in our soul, yet no one ever comes to warm himself at it, and the passers-by see only a wisp of smoke coming through the chimney.

—LETTER TO THEO, JULY 1880

ONE COLD SPRING morning in 1879, twenty-six-year-old Vincent climbed into a basket and was lowered "like a bucket in a well" into the Marcasse, one of the oldest, deepest, and most dangerous coal mines in the Borinage district. Accidents happened there in a dozen different ways. Baskets often tipped or fell. At the bottom, fifteen hundred feet down, daylight dwindled to a point the size of a star in the sky. The miners faced poisoned air, firedamp explosions, water seepage, and cave-ins. Vincent said they got used to it but never lost their horror and fear.

With his vivid visual memory he recalled for Theo the strange subterranean world of the mining tunnels. The lamps of the miners gleamed eerily off the wet stone walls as they worked in chambers extending from the main corridor, some in spaces so tight that they had to use their picks lying down. Young children of both sexes loaded coal into the carts that ran down a rail in a main corridor. Seven old horses stabled at the bottom of the mine pulled the carts to the place where the coal was raised to the surface.

Vincent didn't visit the Marcasse for a tourist thrill. He thought the trip was a necessary part of understanding the desperately poor people of the region, to whom he was supposed to minister: "One might live here for years and never know the real state of things unless one went down in the mines."

He had arrived at his Borinage assignment reasonably well dressed, looking like a "clean Dutchman." He boarded with a local baker and began his duties of teaching and preaching. The miners, "worthy of our respect and sympathy," fascinated him. They lived in small houses—scarcely more than huts— scattered through the woods and along the narrow, twisting old roads. Large chimneys and towering mountains of coal loomed at the mine entrances, which were everywhere.

In his effort to identify with the miners, Vincent moved out of the baker's comfortable house and into a hovel, where he slept on a straw mattress. He gave his warm clothes to the needy, dressed in an old army jacket, and stopped washing the coal dust from his face. One day the baker's wife saw him walking down the street wearing the shabby coat and hat and asked why he had given away all his clothing—"you who are descended from such a noble family of Dutch pastors!"

He answered, "I am a friend of the poor like Jesus was."

She replied bluntly, "You're no longer normal."

Many shared her opinion. Vincent's determination to follow Christ's teachings and give up all he had made people uncomfortable. They regarded him as a kind of holy fool, a man to be respected but not followed. When a mine fire wounded many workers, Vincent tore up his own shirts, soaked them in olive oil, and tended the burns of a man the doctors had given up for dead. The head of the mission criticized his excessive behavior, but Vincent was his usual obstinate self. If he believed he was doing the right thing, other people's opinions didn't matter.

After the trial period, the mission sponsors refused to renew his appointment. They stated that he lacked the gift of oratory; unofficially, Vincent's behavior was judged "too extreme." Desperate and humiliated, he moved to the next town, living on small amounts of money from his father and, when that ran out, on charity.

In early October 1879, Theo, once more enrolled as the family's messenger of reason, visited his down-and-out brother with some practical suggestions. Why didn't Vincent become an engraver of letterheads and cards, or a carpenter's apprentice, a librarian, or even a baker?

Vincent thanked Theo for his advice and reminded him, a little sarcastically, of his attempt to attend theological school. All the wise family discussions and the months of effort had resulted only in failure. It had been the worst, most miserable time of his life. He still shuddered when he thought of the whole absurd undertaking. But at least he had learned something important from the experience—he would have to depend on himself.

After that came silence. For more than nine months Vincent ceased writing to his brother. At one point Mr. van

Gogh, convinced his eldest son was crazy, tried to have him committed to an insane asylum. No one knew how he survived the winter without money or a job. Vincent later blamed his lined face and rough manner on having too often slept outdoors, cold, hungry, and fevered.

What he didn't tell Theo was that he had settled on a new ambition. During the summer of 1879 he wrote to Mr. Tersteeg, his first boss at Goupil, requesting some watercolors, a sketchbook, and two manuals on learning to draw. He claimed to be sketching the miners as a souvenir of his experiences. How could he risk disclosing another plan that might fail?

No one looking at his stiff, lumpy drawings would have predicted success, but Vincent excelled at persistence. He copied all the lessons on anatomy and the human figure in the how-to-draw manuals and tried to apply them to his own sketches of miners and peasants.

With only his books to guide him, Vincent made slow progress. In the winter of 1879–80 he grew depressed. Impulsively he decided to visit the studio of one of his art heroes— the French painter and poet of peasant life Jules Breton. He hoped to meet his idol and even ask for work. That Breton lived in the town of Courrières, a forty-five-mile round trip, was an unimportant detail. Vincent set out on the train but soon found himself on foot. The train didn't go all the way to Courrières, and even if it had, he had only ten francs, too little for a ticket. At least he was a great walker. Walking was free.

When he ran out of money, he exchanged some drawings for crusts of bread. He slept in the open air, in an abandoned wagon that was white with frost in the morning, in a pile of wood, and in a haystack—the most comfortable of his sleeping places, he said, until it began to rain.

When he got to Courrières he never saw the artist. He lacked the nerve to knock on the door and introduce himself, let alone ask for a job. He looked at Breton's new studio, a substantial brick building that seemed alarmingly middle-class to Vincent, who believed a painter of poor people should live like one. He looked in the inn, also built of "repellant" brick, with a mural "of inferior quality" painted on the wall. He looked in the church, where he saw a copy of *Burial of Christ* by Titian that he said had a wonderful tone. And that was all.

He started home again, footsore and weary. The countryside around Courrières comforted him: farms with mossy thatched roofs, peasants driving horses, woodcutters, and women wearing the white caps traditional to that region. From that trip he drew mysterious encouragement. "I said to myself, in spite of everything I shall rise again: I will take up my pencil, which I have forsaken in my great discouragement, and I will go on with my drawing. From that moment everything has seemed transformed for me; and now I have started and my pencil has become somewhat docile, becoming more so every day."

Theo sent fifty francs by way of their parents, which broke the long silence between the two brothers. Vincent wrote reluctantly to thank him. He referred to his solitude in the Borinage as his molting time, comparing it to the time when a bird goes out of sight to change its feathers and emerges renewed. He denied the family's assumption that he simply had been idle. "Such a man does not always know what he could do but he instinctively feels, I am good for something, my life has a purpose after all . . . How could I be useful, of what service can I be?"

Vincent had his own answer to this question. He was no longer religious, if *religious* meant that one participated in what happened in church, but he believed in God. Through his art he aspired to convey that belief and the passionate feeling for humanity that had led him into missionary work. "I always think that the best way to know God is to love many things. Love a friend, a wife, something—whatever you like—you will be on your way to knowing more about Him."

While he didn't exactly announce his ambition to be an artist, his drawing was no secret. In one of his first letters to Theo, he begged him for prints, including anything by Jean-François Millet, a French artist of peasant life he revered almost above all others. He said he had been copying several of Millet's works, including *The Sower,* painted in 1850. "Send me what you can and do not fear for me. If I can only continue to work, somehow or other it will set me right again."

The Borinage had been the place where Vincent hit bottom and finally realized what his life's work would be. Now he had practical problems. Another cold winter approached, when the weather would make it impossible to work outdoors. But the miner's hut where he boarded was too cramped and dank to serve as a studio. So without any discussion he packed up his few belongings and moved again—this time back to Brussels.

He applied to the School of Fine Arts but didn't get the necessary recommendation from the mayor. He also expected that his extended family would be helpful with introductions that might lead to work, perhaps as a draftsman, but there, too, he ran out of luck. His uncles kept their distance. If they knew that people gossiped about Vincent's poverty, it didn't bother them.

Vincent struggled on, trying to live on a pittance from his parents and Theo and spending most of it on art supplies. He survived on coffee, bread, and roasted chestnuts purchased from a street vendor—particularly at the end of the month, before his allowance arrived. Staying in town meant the opportunity to learn from established artists, but eventually Vincent gave in and did what so many others do when they haven't any money. He went home.

In Love

1881–83

*I try to put the same sentiment into the landscape
as I put into the figure.*
—LETTER TO THEO, OCTOBER 1881

THE LARGE, SOLID PARSONAGE at Etten offered the refuge Vincent needed after his hard years in the Borinage. Here he could concentrate on art without worrying about food or a roof over his head. He labored over his drawing, but the stiff figures he produced didn't look too promising. His long-suffering parents made him comfortable and hoped for the best.

Vincent proposed to make a portfolio of "Brabant types"— drawings of peasant figures, faces, and occupations characteristic of the region. Other peasant painters showed their humble subjects at rest or prayer, but Vincent drew men and women working. At first the local gardener, the well digger, and the plowman wanted to wear their Sunday clothes to pose for the artist. It took some persuading on Vincent's part before they consented to be drawn laboring, dressed in everyday clothes and heavy wooden shoes.

No one could accuse Vincent of laziness now. Often the family came downstairs to breakfast to find he had worked through the night. His mother's repeated calls to meals met with an impatient "in a minute" that stretched into hours. Roughly dressed, loaded down with a folding camp stool, easel, and drawing equipment, he became a familiar figure around the village of Etten. The local farmers respected the "queer little fellow." Those who posed for him received drawings in return, to which they paid their highest compliment—"accurate as a photograph." While his parents' friends found him rude, the workingmen of the parish felt he "wasn't the least bit proud," and he was a regular visitor in the houses of the poor, to whom he was as generous as his own poverty enabled him to be.

Mr. and Mrs. van Gogh, reassured that Vincent's skill was improving, wrote optimistic if still worried notes to Theo, who, as usual, heard from all sides of the family. Things might have gone on peaceably for some time if Vincent's newly widowed cousin Kee Vos-Stricker had not arrived to stay at the parsonage with her eight-year-old son. (Her mother and Mrs. van Gogh were sisters.)

Vincent had admired the slightly older Kee and her husband when he lived in Amsterdam, studying for theological school exams. Her father, the distinguished Reverend Mr. Stricker, had been his mentor. Now he spent days walking and talking with Kee and went out of his way to pay attention to her child. She assumed his kindness was to the fatherless boy. Instead he declared his undying love for her. Aghast, Kee cried, "No, never *never*," packed her bags, and fled to her parents' home in Amsterdam, where Vincent peppered her with letters.

Far from sympathizing with their son, Mr. and Mrs. van Gogh scolded him, claiming that Vincent's persistent letters and his refusal to accept Kee's rejections were causing trouble in the family. They accused him of being "indelicate" and "crazy" and of "breaking family ties." How could Vincent, who didn't support himself, take care of a wife and a child?

That, Vincent guessed, was the key opposition to his suit— money. But should he, a man gripped by passion, worry about such a detail? His parents grew so exasperated that they threatened to throw him out of the house. Vincent declined to go, claiming it would block his artistic progress. He begged Theo for train fare to Amsterdam so that he could pursue Kee in person. Theo sent it.

Vincent knocked on the Strickers' door at dinnertime, when he knew the family would be at home. Uncle Stricker let him in but told him that Kee had left the house as soon as he entered it. He admonished Vincent to stop writing to her. Not one to give up so easily, Vincent settled down to plead his case with her elderly parents, as if the strength of his feelings alone would change Kee's mind. As a last resort, he dramatically put his hand in the flame of an oil lamp and said, "Let me see her for as long as I can keep my hand in the flame."

Mr. Stricker blew the flame out. "You will not see her!"

While he stayed in Amsterdam, waiting for a chance to talk to Kee, Vincent didn't lose sight of his artistic goals. The critically and financially successful painter Anton Mauve, his cousin by marriage, lived a short train ride away in The Hague, and Vincent went to visit. Mauve looked at Vincent's

latest drawing and said, "I always thought you rather dull but now I see it isn't true," which Vincent took as high praise. He promised that when Vincent was ready he would help him.

After three days Vincent gave up the struggle with Kee's family and returned to the parsonage at Etten. He never saw Kee again. Bitterly he blamed his parents for his unhappiness, and on Christmas Day the tensions between father and son exploded. The immediate cause was Vincent's refusal to go to church. When his father insisted, Vincent wrathfully denounced the hypocrisy of organized religion. One angry word led to another, and Mr. van Gogh, who could be as pigheaded as his infuriating son, demanded he leave the house "immediately." This time Vincent went, abandoning his dream of finishing the Brabant portfolio.

With no other place to go, he turned up, a few months earlier than expected, on Mauve's doorstep. The worldly artist advised the scruffy-looking Vincent to dress a little better so that he could go out socially and meet people who would be useful to him. Then he generously lent him enough money to set up a modest studio.

Vincent couldn't afford to live in one of The Hague's imposing neighborhoods dotted with parks and lakes. Instead he rented a single room with an alcove in a ramshackle building on a cinder path. The room had a view of the railroad sheds. Mauve's loan covered the purchase of a sturdy table and a bed. Vincent decorated the walls with a mixture of his own drawings and illustrations from magazines and even purchased a few bulbs in pots. Proudly he detailed his housekeeping to Theo, inviting him to visit anytime.

Mauve, one of the leaders of the Hague school of artists, was a prickly character who refused to take students, but he consented to teach Vincent, perhaps partly because his wife,

Jet, was the niece of Vincent's mother. Vincent settled in to learn as much as possible, and he rapidly progressed under Mauve's guidance.

Art was the one area in which Vincent tried to control his temper. Not that he didn't have his moments. Mauve started him drawing in charcoal and crayon, and Vincent admitted to Theo that he had become so impatient, he'd stamped on the charcoal stick. After his tantrum was over, he'd picked up the stick, determined to master the technique: "If it were so easy, there would be no fun in it."

At Goupil in Paris, Theo had received a promotion and a raise, so he gave his brother a small but regular allowance, which Vincent tended to spend immediately. To help out, Theo arranged with Mr. Tersteeg, the head of Goupil in The Hague, to lend him money from time to time. Vincent was outraged to find that the loan came with a stern lecture. Tersteeg held firm opinions, and as a friend of the family, he believed his duty lay in reprimanding their black sheep. "You are no artist. You started too late. You should earn your own living. You failed before and you'll fail again." Vincent raged that he'd rather go without dinner than ever ask anything of Tersteeg again.

Shortly after this meeting, Vincent's uncle Cor, one of the art dealer uncles, stopped by the studio to suggest it was time that Vincent "earned his bread." Uncle Cor looked at his nephew's recent sketches and, to Vincent's amazed pleasure, bought three views of The Hague's historic district as part of a twelve-drawing order. Vincent set the price at two and a half guilders each and excitedly promised Theo that with a few more customers like this, he'd be able to support himself. Unfortunately the drawings of the gasworks and the iron foundry Vincent soon produced were not the pretty trifles Uncle Cor had in mind. His gallery's customers wanted picturesque images as souvenirs—not scenes of the city's grungy industrial outskirts. Uncle Cor tried again with a very specific order, but Vincent resisted painting lightweight tableaus, claiming such drawings hurt his progress as an artist. He gave his uncle renderings of a fish-drying barn and a carpenter's yard and laundry. Uncle Cor pronounced them unsalable and offered him no more assignments.

All Vincent's relationships in The Hague were becoming strained. Cor had written him off. Tersteeg, aggressively critical, called his work charmless. Even Mauve, who had taught him many important things and introduced him to watercolor technique, now seemed unreasonable. He instructed Vincent to practice drawing the human figure from plaster casts of Greek and Roman statues, a task Vincent loathed. Vincent said, "I kept quiet, but when I got home I was so angry that I threw those poor plaster casts into a coal bin, and they were smashed to pieces. And I thought, I will draw from those casts only when they become whole and white again and when there are no more hands and feet of living beings to draw from." On hearing this, Mauve, who also had a hot temper, told Vincent to stay away for two months.

After the two months passed, Vincent tracked Mauve down and asked him to visit. Mauve refused. "I will certainly not come to see you, that's all over." He then said, "You have a vicious character."

Vincent wrote asking Theo if he had any insight into why every hand was against him. In the next sentence he admitted the truth. He was living with a woman named Christine Hoornik (also called Sien). Until he met her she had added to the tiny income she earned from sewing and taking in laundry by working as a prostitute. When he first picked her up, she was sick and pregnant. He saw her as a wounded dove, but to those who viewed her without Vincent's compassion, she was a tough, uneducated woman of the streets, with a face scarred by smallpox, a grating voice, a five-year-old daughter, and a grasping family.

Vincent had a dozen deeply human reasons to involve himself with someone his middle-class world found depraved. The biggest one seems to have been his need to love and be loved after his shattering rejection by Kee. Sien, sick and vulnerable, filled a terrible, lonely space in his life. True, she had a bad temper, but he said it helped her understand his own outbursts. He yearned to save her. "Am I free to marry—yes or no? Am I free to put on a workman's clothes and live like a workman—yes or no? Whom am I responsible to? Who will try to force me?"

He refused to recognize that his association with Sien had created ill will in two valuable former supporters—Tersteeg and Mauve—and he swore that Sien helped him in his work by cleaning his studio and modeling for him.

Theo was not overjoyed at Vincent's news, but he did not cut off his support. However, he warned his brother that when their parents heard of Vincent's affair, they might once more try to have him confined to a madhouse. Who but an insane person could behave so disgracefully? Vincent sturdily resisted. It would not be so easy to have him declared incompetent.

Sien brought her infant son home from the hospital to a new studio—all arranged at Theo's expense. Vincent had labored to build partitions and hang curtains, making a safe nest for what he referred to as his "little family." Elated at the domestic reality of a cradle with a baby in it, he settled in to work harder than ever. Sien and her two children at least gave him the illusion of the family life he longed for, and he responded with many sensitive drawings that reflected his attachment. "Who am I in most people's eyes? A nonentity, or an eccentric and disagreeable man—in short the lowest of the low. . . . I want to progress so far that people will say of my work, He feels deeply, he feels tenderly—not withstanding my so-called roughness, perhaps even because of it."

The men and women who lived in the local poorhouse also caught his artistic attention. Most were old, with no families to take care of them. Vincent paid some to pose for a group of drawings he called "Heads of the People," after an English series he admired. Believing as he did in the power of art to both uplift and console, he wanted the prints to be sold cheaply to decorate workingmen's homes. Like the rest of Vincent's proposals for making money, this didn't happen, but he did make some lithographs and was proud when the printer's helpers asked for copies to hang on their walls.

Since he first picked up a pencil in the Borinage, he had focused on drawing, persuaded that it was the foundation of everything. Now, after several years of strenuous effort, he felt the time had come to start painting, and his letters gloried in his newfound pleasure. He set to work learning theories of color with the same intensity he had spent on drawing.

Vincent's painting technique was largely self-taught, the result of trial and error, but he was not a naive painter. One day as he was working on a painting in an autumn forest, he discovered that if he squeezed the paint directly from the tube onto the canvas, the thick paint made the trees look rooted in nature: "I see that nature has told me something, has spoken to me, and that I have put it down in shorthand."

In a letter Vincent wrote in August 1883, he added a

startling postscript. He said that given his health, his body should hold up for another six to ten years, during which he hoped to accomplish something "full of heart and love." He didn't expect to live longer.

Sien hardly was mentioned. Vincent reported that his life with her was not "moonlight and roses but something prosaic like a Monday morning." Now that her baby had been born and her health was coming back, Sien was less "a tame dove" and more a difficult woman who didn't find it easy, or worthwhile, to change her ways. What Theo sent barely supported four people, especially when one of them had a constant need for expensive art supplies. Sien's family urged a return to prostitution, where she could earn more than she did posing for a poor artist.

In the end, the pressures on them were too strong. Vincent and Sien sadly agreed to part. She said she planned to work as a laundress, doing other people's washing and ironing. He didn't believe she would remain virtuous, but defended her to his family, saying, "She has never seen what is *good* so how can she be good." He gave Sien what he could—a tender farewell and a piece of his best canvas to make clothes for the children. With that he set out on a new artistic journey.

His destination was Drenthe, a flat, windswept province in the north of Holland. It had been recommended by a friend as a place where the scenery inspired painters. Blank spaces on the map, no towns for miles, and notations indicating peat fields lured Vincent with the promise of sweeping landscapes and big, exciting skies.

Visually inspiring as Drenthe might be in autumn, it also was wet, bleak, and windy. The other artists who painted there had gone home at summer's end, leaving Vincent in the company of farmers and sheep. He couldn't find art supplies and had to order them from The Hague. As fall gave way to winter, he grew lonelier.

Most days it was too cold to paint outdoors and too cramped to paint indoors. Restless, with nothing to do except write long letters to Theo about art and the scenery, Vincent loaded up his paints, luggage, and all the canvases he could carry. Then he hoisted his bundles and walked to the train station—six hours across a snowy heath. With some idea of making a visit to his parents before starting out again, he went to their new parsonage in Nuenen, another small town in Brabant. His visit would last two years.

Vincent the Dog
1883 – 85

*I am getting to be like a dog, I feel that the future will
probably make me more ugly and rough, and I
foresee that "a certain poverty" will be my
fate, but, but, but, I shall be a painter.*

—LETTER TO THEO, DECEMBER 1883

VINCENT CAME HOME ready to give his parents another
chance to do the right thing. If only his father would apologize for throwing him out of the house, they could all settle down to the important business of Vincent's becoming
an artist. Mr. van Gogh didn't see it that way. He and
Vincent's mother welcomed their thirty-year-old problem
child, but they were ambivalent at the prospect of having
him back in the nest. After a few days Vincent wrote humorously yet bitterly to Theo, comparing himself to a
stray dog.

Dear brother,

I feel what Father and Mother think of me instinctively (I do not say intelligently).

They feel the same dread of taking me in the house as they would about taking in a big rough dog. He would run into the room with wet paws—and he is so rough. He will be in everybody's way. And he barks so loud. In short he is a foul beast.

Vincent's strong sense of injustice blinded him to his parents' understandable worries. In a small, rural nineteenth-century town such as Nuenen, the arrival of the new pastor's nonchurchgoing son, a son who dressed like a tramp and painted outdoors in all weather, gave Mr. van Gogh's parishioners plenty of juicy gossip to discuss over dinner. If Vincent had ever possessed any social skills, he no longer bothered to use them. When visitors came at the family mealtime, he left the table and ate his bread in a corner, scowling over a painting in progress. People who peered curiously over his shoulder while he painted outdoors were ordered to go away.

There were a few tense weeks, but in the end his parents' kindheartedness won out. They cared about their complicated boy. After some negotiation, they gave him the use of the laundry room for a studio and fixed it up to be as comfortable as a small room located between the sewer and the coal storage pit could be. Mr. van Gogh wrote to Theo that "with real courage we undertake this new experiment and we intend to leave him perfectly free in his peculiarities of dress etc. The people here have seen him anyhow, and though it is a pity he is so reserved we cannot change the fact of his being eccentric."

Vincent's relationship with his family was improved by an accident. Mrs. van Gogh stepped off a train, fell, and broke her leg just below the hip. The nursing skills Vincent had learned in the Borinage surprised his parents and bettered their opinion of him. While the most personal nursing duties fell on Vincent's youngest sister, Wil, his tender and competent care of his ailing mother astounded everyone.

He had reached a truce with his parents, but his relationship with Theo was now rocky. Vincent attacked his brother about their monetary arrangements and accused him of making no attempt to sell the paintings and of breaking up the relationship with Sien "with a little tug at the financial bridle." He wrote angrily, "A wife you cannot give me, a child you cannot give me, work you cannot give me. Money, yes. But what good is it to me if I must do without the rest?"

The quarrel finally led to a new understanding. Theo sent Vincent 150 francs per month as a salary. Vincent was free to spend the money any way he wished. In return he sent Theo his paintings, to sell or keep as he chose. From that point onward Vincent regarded Theo as a business partner as well as his closest friend. Theo's job was to provide support and art materials, Vincent's to make paintings.

The area around Nuenen offered plenty of subjects to interest him. He had first been fascinated by weavers while he was living in the Borinage. Now he spent days crouched in the corners of the local weavers' huts, drawing. He identified with the humble, solitary craftsmen who looked trapped inside the intricate wooden looms. Their livelihood was vanishing as more and more fabric was manufactured with new power looms in large, industrialized mills.

With his finances stabilized, Vincent moved his studio from the family laundry room to two larger rooms rented to him by the sexton of the village's Catholic church. This annoyed his father, who got along fine with his Catholic neighbors but didn't wish his son to be so closely associated with them. And it equally annoyed the priest, who didn't like having an artist's studio so near the church.

The painting went well in the new space until Vincent unwittingly created a fresh uproar. Next door to the parsonage lived the very respectable Begemann family, including the never-married forty-five-year-old daughter, Margo, a hopeless spinster by the standards of the time. She worked in the family linen business but found time to help out most of the neighbors, including Mrs. van Gogh with her broken leg. Vincent, poor, outlandish, and more than ten years younger than Margo, hardly qualified as Prince Charming, but the two lonely people cared for each other. They agreed to marry.

Margo's three sisters and sister-in-law ruthlessly objected to her romance with the pastor's peculiar son, humiliating her past the breaking point. Margo snapped. While she and Vincent were out walking in the fields, she sank to the ground, exclaiming, "I too have loved at last!"

At first Vincent thought Margo had fainted, and then, fearing the worst, demanded to know if she had swallowed something. She screamed, "Yes!" and admitted she had taken poison. He promptly ordered her to put her finger down her throat. Then he found her brother and rushed to the nearest town for a doctor. Margo went away for a long rest. Vincent visited her, but given Margo's fragile emotional condition, marriage didn't seem wise. He said that she had spent too long under the domination of her dispiriting family, and he compared her to a valuable old violin that had been abused and badly mended.

Most of the neighbors blamed Vincent for the drama and refused to visit the parsonage as long as he lived there, which upset his mother. He was too busy to worry about it. To help his finances, he accepted three pupils, who paid him in tubes of paint so that he could work from morning till night without running out of materials. His students found him an unusual teacher. He planned his canvas carefully, and then, without drawing, painted quickly and confidently from one side of the canvas to the other, using a large brush, his fingers, and even his fingernails to get the effects he sought. When his pupils commented that what he did was contrary to academic technique, he shouted, "I scoff at your technique."

His chaotic studio was crammed with paintings and drawings mounted on every available wall space, many of them strong heads of men and women with clownish turned-up noses, protruding cheekbones, and large ears. There were a few frayed chairs, all kinds of mosses and plants, stuffed birds, farm tools, costumes for his models, a stove surrounded by a heap of ashes that went untouched, and a cupboard full of at least thirty different birds' nests. He paid the boys in the neighborhood to bring him the nests, which he painted and compared to the small, cozy peasants' houses.

Vincent's painting and his confidence had improved tremendously, but his disposition had not. Both parents complained of his behavior. In March 1885 Mr. van Gogh wrote to Theo, "This morning I talked things over with Vincent; he was in a kind mood and said there was no particular reason for his being depressed. May he meet with success anyhow." These were his last written words about his son. Three days later he went out for a walk on the heath, came home, and collapsed in the doorway of the house. He was carried inside, but it was too late. There was nothing anyone could do. Vincent's father was dead at age sixty-three.

The van Goghs had been a devoted couple for forty-four years. The grieving Mrs. van Gogh was allowed to stay on in the parsonage for a year, but Vincent's sisters asked him to move out and leave their mother in peace. Vincent, not admitting how hurt he was, took up residence in his studio by the Catholic church.

As usual, he kept busy working. He put his faith in a large painting that had preoccupied him for months, one that he felt had "energy." The scene depicted a peasant family sitting around a table in a dark room lit by a single overhead lamp. Vincent wanted to represent an attitude and a way of life, not an individual family, so he named his painting *The Potato Eaters*, after the evening meal that waited in front of them.

He painted it in less than a month but said he had spent the whole winter on studies of the hands and heads, completing several oil sketches and a lithograph before beginning the final canvas: "I have such a feel of the thing that I can literally dream it." Vincent's sense of identification with these laborers, his belief in their simplicity and goodness, is evident in the work. "I have tried to emphasize that these people eating their potatoes in the lamplight, have dug the earth with those very hands they put in the dish, and so it speaks of manual labor and how they have honestly earned their food."

The color scheme was dark, his favorite bistre and bitumen heightened with gold. The heads he painted "the color of a very dusty potato, unpeeled of course." He left the brushwork purposely rough. "It would be wrong to give a peasant picture a certain conventional smoothness. If a peasant picture smells of bacon, smoke, potato steam—that's not unhealthy . . . to be perfumed is not what a peasant picture needs . . . We must continue to give something real and honest."

Vincent sent Theo a preliminary print of the painting and many sketches, encouraging him to hold on to all of the drawings and studies—otherwise they'd have to buy them back when he became famous. He also advised retaining the best paintings for what he referred to as his oeuvre, the body of work on which he expected to be favorably judged.

The Potato Eaters now is considered one of the great paintings of the nineteenth century, but at the time Theo and others who saw it did not respond to it with the praise Vincent knew it deserved. In spite of a few faults in composition, which he readily admitted, he had painted a masterpiece. But with lukewarm enthusiasm Theo informed him that the Impressionists had introduced a much lighter palette than Vincent's blacks and "soapy greens." To be a success in Paris, he was going to have to lighten his colors. Vincent wrote back that he had heard of the Impressionists, although he had never seen any of their work. He couldn't visualize what Theo was talking about.

In Nuenen he faced a new dilemma. The local priest, who had never liked Vincent or his studio, denounced him as a bad influence and forbade the parishioners to pose. In fact, the priest offered to pay them not to. Vincent hadn't done anything wrong, but with his models no longer available, it was time to move on. He had learned much in the country; now he needed the city—to see paintings and to talk to other artists.

Before leaving Nuenen, Vincent gave one of his favorite paintings, an autumn landscape, to a friend and pupil, Anton Kerssemakers. When Anton pointed out that he hadn't signed the painting, Vincent said he might someday, but "actually it isn't necessary, they will surely recognize my work later on and write about me when I am dead and gone."

Vincent relocated to the bustling city of Antwerp, Belgium, where he anticipated a market for his work. Here he took a room over a paint dealer's shop for twenty-five francs a month. He rented a stove and a lamp and settled in to explore big-city life. Antwerp was a busy international port on the river Schelde. Vincent never got tired of walking the streets and looking at the people. With Antwerp's museum, full of great art, as well as its entertaining cafés, music halls, and bars, there was plenty to catch Vincent's attention. In a shop near the waterfront he discovered inexpensive Japanese prints for the first time. The simplicity of their flat shapes seemed very modern to him, and he decorated the walls of his small room with these exotic images of life in Japan.

He had several schemes for making money—painting portraits, selling drawings—that came to nothing. A hundred and fifty francs a month didn't go far in an expensive town, and he came very close to starvation. As usual, he splurged on art supplies and survived on bread and coffee. His health deteriorated so much that it affected his painting, and he began to lose his teeth. And while he found people to draw, nude models still eluded him. They had been out of the question in straitlaced Nuenen, but in Antwerp, hoping for an opportunity, he enrolled in the art academy, where luckily classes were free.

He must have been a strange sight. Other students recalled a laughable figure with paint-stained workman's clothes and a ratty fur cap worn indoors and out. Vincent didn't care about their laughter. He had rejected everything about the life he had been born into and was pleased when people mistook him for an ironworker or a bargeman just off the river. In class he flung himself down in front of the canvas and put on the paint so quickly and heavily that it dripped on the floor. The outraged teacher asked who he was. "Vincent, a Dutchman," he replied. The teacher refused to correct such sloppy work and demoted him to a lower class.

Vincent went quietly. He was there to paint the models,

not to have arguments. He claimed he learned more from watching the other students than from the faculty. He didn't respect his teachers' methods, and he painted as he wished, not as they instructed. Unimpressed by his originality, the school once more demoted him, this time into the beginners' class. He left before he found out.

Desperate to see the artistic developments in Paris, he kept badgering Theo to let him come. His brother put him off, asking Vincent to wait until he moved to a bigger apartment. In the meantime, Theo suggested, their mother and sisters in Nuenen needed help moving to their new home. Vincent refused. Visiting Nuenen would be money badly spent. "In a time of financial crisis like the present, money is what ammunition is to a soldier in a hostile country—don't let's waste our powder." He translated his point of view into action. Leaving a stack of unpaid bills behind, he boarded the night train to Paris.

A Country Bumpkin in Paris

1886–87

I am not an adventurer by choice as by fate and feeling nowhere so much myself a stranger as in my family and country.
—LETTER TO ENGLISH ARTIST HORACE LEVENS, SEPTEMBER 1886

ON A SCRAP of paper torn from his sketchbook, Vincent dashed off a note to Theo. "My dear Theo, Do not be cross with me for having come all at once like this: I have thought about it so much, and I believe that in this way we shall save time. . . . We'll fix things up, you'll see." He probably avoided going straight to Goupil et Cie, where Theo worked, for fear of running into his former bosses, so he sent an errand boy with the message. Then he settled into a gallery of the Louvre to wait for his brother. He chose to meet Theo in the room where the most important paintings were hung, to let him know he was determined to be taken seriously as an artist.

Vincent arrived in Paris a country bumpkin and found himself in the red-hot center of the art world. The older artists working there, such as Manet, Monet, Renoir, and Degas, were the recognized leaders of Impressionism, a movement that had burst on the Paris art scene in the 1870s. Vincent thought himself an expert on painting, but when he saw what the Impressionists were doing, he realized how much he had to learn. Their light-filled, color-drenched canvases soon would turn the sober Dutch palette of *The Potato Eaters* upside down.

Theo's apartment was only a ten-minute walk from the gallery. That it was too small may have been the reason Theo wasn't overjoyed when his brother showed up so unexpectedly. At the same time, Theo felt lonely and out of place in sophisticated Paris. Like Vincent, who described himself as a boy from Brabant, Theo was happier in the countryside than in the big city. So having his brother and best friend around to share his life might have been a relief. At least now there would be only one rent to pay. After several months they moved to a larger apartment on boulevard Montmartre, even closer to Goupil and near the artist Fernand Corman's studio, where Vincent immediately enrolled to study figure drawing.

One section of Montmartre, at the foot of the famous hill known as the Butte-Montmartre, was covered with vegetable gardens and a few disused windmills. The construction of the white church Sacré-Coeur was just under way. The other section pulsed with lively bistros and cafés, including the popular dance hall Windmill of the Galette, which Vincent soon painted. From the brothers' third-floor apartment he could look out over the tiled rooftops of Paris with their orange chimneys and glass skylights.

Vincent and Theo's new home had three large rooms, a small side room, where Vincent slept, and a kitchen. The living room was decorated with an antique wood cabinet belonging to Theo, a sofa, and a big stove, since both brothers disliked the cold.

Vincent adjusted to life in Paris with renewed energy and enthusiasm. He was eager to leave behind the conservative rules and taboos of his Dutch homeland and to embrace the freedom and daring that France offered him. He wrote his letters in French and replaced the old blue smock and fur cap he had worn in Antwerp with an artistic felt hat, a colorful scarf, and a suit. He painted himself in this new outfit, looking out at the viewer with a steady gaze. Vincent did twenty-five self-portraits in Paris, more than in any other period of his career. His studies of his own image, seen in a mirror, show his preoccupation with self-examination. He would try on different roles, from coarse peasant to urbane gentleman, from plain farmer to solemn artist.

His health, both mental and physical, continued to worry his family. To his mother's relief, he had some much-needed dental work done, as he had lost almost all his teeth. Theo wrote to Mrs. van Gogh, "You would not recognize Vincent, he has changed so much. . . . The doctor says he has quite recovered."

Theo's position as an art dealer and patron of the Impressionist painters gave Vincent access to the art world of Paris. He also met many of the younger artists then considered avant-garde—Paul Signac, Henri de Toulouse-Lautrec, and Paul Gauguin, to name only a few. In the galleries and cafés around Montmartre they gathered to smoke their pipes, listen to *les chanteuses*, the female ballad singers, and drink absinthe, a strong toxic liquor. Theo told the family that not a day went by without an invitation for Vincent to visit a well-known painter's studio.

The French Impressionists totally changed Vincent's way of thinking about painting. Impressionism, with its pastel colors and disconnected brushstrokes, aimed to convey a sense of spontaneity, to be a record of a fleeting scene. At first Vincent wasn't sure he liked their bright colors. He preferred the gray tones of painters such as Mauve, with whom he was more familiar. But gradually over the course of the summer he began to replace the dull grays with stronger colors, experimenting by painting a series of flowers. Since he couldn't afford to pay models, friends in the neighborhood would bring him fresh bouquets to paint instead.

In his first months in Paris, he studied figure drawing at Corman's studio, where an artist he'd met in Amsterdam had trained. Vincent gave up the peasant themes he'd committed himself to in Holland and joined Corman's other students in working from live models as well as drawing from plaster casts. He had come a long way from the young man who had smashed Mauve's casts rather than copy them. Now he admitted that there were things to be learned from studying classical models.

Corman, a little man with a long, thin face and a pointy chin, stood on a ladder at the front of the studio, working on his large historical canvases of prehistoric lake dwellers and cavemen, while the students sat at their easels at the other end, painting the model. Vincent's new friend, the eighteen-year-old painter and poet Emile Bernard, would find him there long after the rest of the students had left, patiently trying to draw the contours of a plaster cast. Vincent worked with such intensity that he rubbed holes in the paper from erasing over and over. He disciplined himself for the sake of his craft, but he was far from mellow. His frequent outbursts, as well as the odd color combinations he preferred, caused the younger students to make fun of him behind his back. But they were civil to him; after all, his brother Theo was a well-known art dealer. When Vincent became excited, he had a way of spitting out a string of sentences in French, Dutch, and English, looking back at people over his shoulder and hissing through his remaining teeth. The students admitted being impressed by his painting of a pair of worn workman's boots against a drab background. Vincent said he didn't need to paint figures to express the sadness he saw in the world.

Not too surprisingly, Vincent wasn't a fan of Corman's work, and after a few months he abruptly quit. For the time being he gave up on painting nudes from live models. What did come out of that brief experience was two new artist friends—Emile Bernard and Henri de Toulouse-Lautrec.

Vincent's father,
Theodorus van Gogh.
Van Gogh Museum
(Vincent van Gogh
Foundation),
Amsterdam.

Vincent's mother,
Anna Cornelia
van Gogh-Carbentus.
Van Gogh Museum
(Vincent van Gogh
Foundation),
Amsterdam.

Vincent at age
thirteen, in 1866.
Van Gogh Museum
(Vincent van Gogh
Foundation),
Amsterdam.

The house in Groot-Zundert where Vincent was born.
Van Gogh Museum (Vincent van Gogh Foundation), Amsterdam.

Square in Ramsgate. (Drawing from letter 67.) 1876.
Pencil, pen and ink on paper. Van Gogh Museum (Vincent van Gogh Foundation), Amsterdam.

Sien with Cigar, Sitting on the Floor by the Stove. 1882.
Pencil, black chalk, pen and brush (sepia), white wash heightened with white Ingres
paper. 18 x 22 in. (45.4 x 56 cm). Kröller-Müller Museum, Otterlo.

The Potato Eaters. 1885. Oil on canvas. 32 1/4 x 44 7/8 in. (82 x 114 cm).
Van Gogh Museum (Vincent van Gogh Foundation), Amsterdam.

Vincent's Bedroom at Arles. 1888. Oil on canvas. 28 3/8 x 35 7/16 in. (72 x 90 cm).
Musée d'Orsay, Paris.

Vincent's House in Arles, the "Yellow House." 1888. Oil on canvas. 28 3/8 x 36 in. (72 x 91.5 cm). Van Gogh Museum (Vincent van Gogh Foundation), Amsterdam.

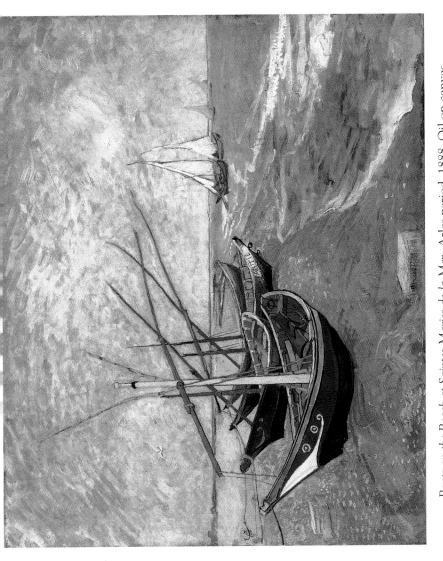

Boats on the Beach at Saintes-Maries-de-la-Mer. Arles period, 1888. Oil on canvas.
25 x 31 7/8 in. (65 x 81.5 cm).

Van Gogh Museum (Vincent van Gogh Foundation), Amsterdam.

The Night Café (Le Café de Nuit). Arles, 1888. Oil on canvas. 28½ x 36¼ in. (72.4 x 92.1 cm). Yale University Art Gallery. Bequest of Stephen Carlton Clark, B.A., 1903.

Harvest at Le Crau. Arles, 1888. Oil on canvas. 28¾ x 36¼ in. (73 x 92 cm).
Van Gogh Museum (Vincent van Gogh Foundation), Amsterdam.

Postman Joseph Roulin. Arles, 1888. Oil on canvas. 32 x 2511/16 in. (81.2 x 65.3 cm).
Museum of Fine Arts, Boston. Gift of Robert Treat Paine II, 1935.

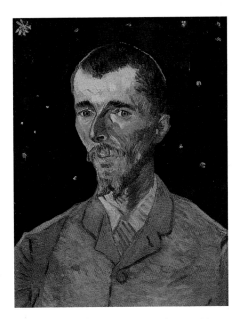

Le Père Tanguy. Arles, 1887.
Oil on canvas.
361/4 x 291/2 in. (92 x 75 cm).
Musée Rodin, Paris.

Portrait of Eugène Boch. Arles, 1888.
Oil on canvas.
235/8 x 173/4 in. (60 x 45 cm).
Musée d'Orsay, Paris.

Portrait of Dr. Paul Gachet. Auvers, 1890.
Oil on canvas.
263/4 x 221/2 in. (68 x 57 cm).
Musée d'Orsay, Paris.

Vase with Sunflowers. Arles, 1889.
Oil on canvas.
37 7/8 x 28 3/4 in. (95 x 73 cm).
Van Gogh Museum (Vincent van Gogh Foundation), Amsterdam.

Wheatfield with a Reaper. St. Rémy, 1889. Oil on canvas. 283/4 x 361/4 in. (73 x 92 cm). Van Gogh Museum (Vincent van Gogh Foundation), Amsterdam.

Lullaby: Madame Augustine Roulin Rocking a Cradle (La Berceuse). Arles, 1889.
Oil on canvas.
36 1/2 x 28 11/16 in. (92.7 x 72.8 cm).
Museum of Fine Arts, Boston. Bequest of John T. Spaulding, 1948.

Road with Cypress and Star. St. Rémy, 1890.
Oil on canvas. 361/4 x 283/4 in. (92 x 73 cm).
Kröller-Müller Museum, Otterlo.

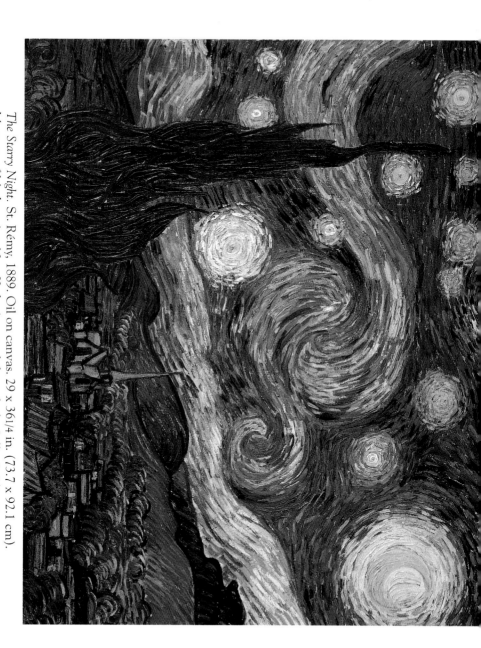

The Starry Night. St. Rémy, 1889. Oil on canvas. 29 x 36¼ in. (73.7 x 92.1 cm). Museum of Modern Art, New York. Acquired through the Lillie P. Bliss Bequest.

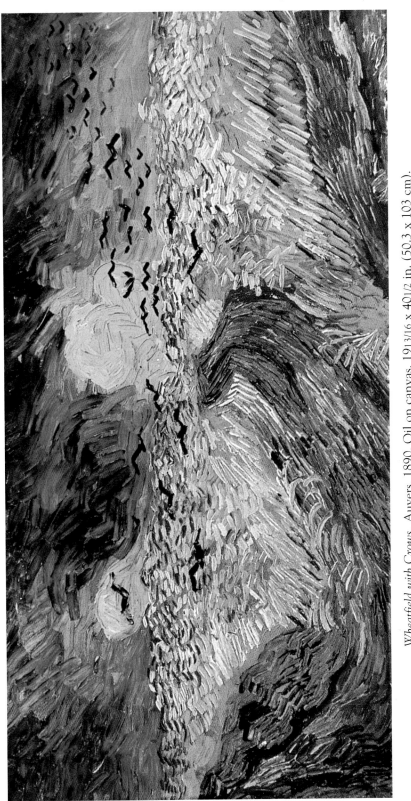

Wheatfield with Crows. Auvers, 1890. Oil on canvas. 19 13/16 x 40 1/2 in. (50.3 x 103 cm). Van Gogh Museum (Vincent van Gogh Foundation), Amsterdam.

Self-Portrait at the Easel. Paris, 1888.
255/8 x 201/8 in. (65 x 50.5 cm).
Van Gogh Museum (Vincent van Gogh Foundation), Amsterdam.

Vincent and Friends
1887–88

I know big long canvases are difficult to sell, but later on people will see that there is open air in them and that they are good-humored.
—LETTER TO THEO, PARIS, SUMMER 1887

TOULOUSE-LAUTREC WAS Vincent's complete opposite in background and personality. A French aristocrat, he had a penchant for the wild Parisian life and the drinking that went with it. He loved to dress in costume and play practical jokes. His striking posters advertising music halls appeared on street corners and kiosks all around Paris. Born with a congenital weakness that affected his bones, as an adult he stood only four feet, eight inches tall, with short legs, a man's torso, and a huge head. He hobbled about on a hollow cane filled with brandy. The awkward, too-serious Dutchman was attracted to Toulouse-Lautrec, who compensated for his small body with a larger-than-life personality. And Vincent, sensitive to human suffering of all kinds, had deep sympathy for the younger artist's affliction. Toulouse-Lautrec's studio was a meeting place for many well-known artists and critics. Week after week Vincent would visit, standing shyly at the edge of the room, clutching his canvas, waiting for someone to comment. He was always disappointed.

In Paris, as he had in Antwerp, Vincent learned more about painting from observing other painters than from the teachers. He imitated the style of the Impressionist painters he admired, such as Claude Monet. Camille Pissarro, who took on the role of mentor to Vincent and the younger artists, explained how to combine colors with a series of short brushstrokes. From the artist Paul Signac Vincent learned the color theories of the Pointillists, who systematically placed dots of complementary colors such as yellow and blue side by side, instead of mixing them, to make green. But the painstaking effort of painting little dots of color lost its appeal for Vincent, who turned the Pointillist brushstroke into longer dashes.

He and Signac often hiked to the suburbs of Paris to paint. One day, carrying their paints, brushes, easels, and canvases slung over their backs, they spent the day working on the banks of the Seine with a view of Paris in the distance. Vincent divided a large canvas into squares so that he could make more than one study at a time, filling the spaces with boats, houses, and restaurants shaded by oleanders. They worked all day and walked back to Paris at dusk. In his blue plumber's blouse, the sleeves dotted with paint he'd daubed there as a test, Vincent talked nonstop to Signac all the way home. Gesturing this way and that with his newly painted canvas, he doused himself and passersby with streaks of wet paint.

He also took excursions to paint in the nearby town of Asnières, where Emile Bernard lived with his parents. There he argued with Emile's father, who, Vincent said, should be more supportive of his son's career as an artist, even if he earned no money. The slender, dark-haired Bernard had a streak of originality and daring that Vincent declared should be nourished.

This proved to be an intense learning period for Vincent, who resolved to master new techniques as well as to develop his own style. He had started collecting brightly colored Japanese woodcuts in Antwerp and, now sure of their worth, had amassed more than two hundred to hang on the walls of his and Theo's apartment. He studied their colorful decorative designs, and a number of his paintings at the time incorporated images from the prints. In his portrait of the paint store owner Père Tanguy, Vincent painted him facing the viewer against an imaginary backdrop of Japanese seasonal scenes and costumed figures instead of in a typical Parisian setting.

In Tanguy's little store the young, progressive artists met to talk and buy paints. If they were broke, the old man, a peasant from Brittany, obliged them by trading supplies for their finished artworks, which he put all over the store. Vincent was glad when Tanguy hung a painting of his in the window but complained that Tanguy's "old witch of a wife" tried to prevent her husband from giving Vincent the canvases he couldn't afford to buy. After Vincent's death, Tanguy sold one of his still lifes to a critic for exactly forty-two francs. When the man asked why not forty or fifty, Tanguy replied, "I looked up what poor van Gogh owed me when he died. It was forty-two francs. Now I have got it back."

Thanks to his visits to Tanguy's shop and the studios, Vincent had become well known in the bohemian artists' community of Paris. His favorite hangout was the Café du Tambourin, where tambourines decorated with pictures and poems by the patrons hung on the walls, and where the tables were shaped like drums. Vincent, who preferred this unpretentious atmosphere to that of the staid Goupil gallery, attempted to arrange small exhibitions there. He did a show of Japanese prints and hung his own paintings on the walls as well. However, this venture ended one night after he picked a fight with a waiter who was jealous of Vincent's romance with the owner, Agostina Segatori. The fiery Agostina booted Vincent out. When he returned a few months later, he found she'd gone out of business, and he had to fight to retrieve his paintings, some of which had been peddled as waste canvas.

He organized another exhibit of 150 works at a restaurant on the avenue de Clichy, where Bernard sold his first painting. Most of the artists, even those who were middle-class and had family support, like Vincent, lived hand to mouth; therefore they appreciated his efforts. Each in their own way tried to break from the Impressionists, to create a "modern" style that went beyond an "impression of the moment." Vincent referred to these young artists as the painters of the *petit boulevard*. (The *grand boulevard* signified the more established Impressionists.) His friends regarded his work with interest, and his opinions were valued in spite of his unruly personality. At last he'd found the camaraderie for which he'd searched vainly in The Hague and Antwerp.

However, Vincent's habit of drinking and carousing all night in the bars of Montmartre began to take its toll. Theo complained in letters home to their sister Wil that Vincent was driving him crazy. His unkempt appearance, untidiness in the apartment, and bullying temper made it impossible for Theo to invite anyone to visit. He left tubes of paint around and used Theo's socks to wipe off a canvas. He marched into Theo's bedroom at all hours with insults and demands. Theo tried to be tolerant, but it was exasperating to live with such an ungrateful brother. Vincent harassed him for money, yet never wanted to earn any on his own. He didn't seem to care whether he sold his paintings, preferring to hoard them or to trade for his friends' pictures. Vincent said his reason for trading was to build a collection that someday might be valuable. If Theo disagreed with any of his whims, Vincent would follow him around the apartment, puffing on his pipe, arguing incessantly.

Theo wrote to their sister Wil, "It is as if he had two persons in him—one marvelously gifted, delicate and tender, and the other egotistical and hardhearted. They present themselves in turn, so that one hears him talk first one way, then in the other, and this always with arguments which are now all for, all against the same point. It is a pity that he is his own enemy, for he makes life hard not only for others but for himself."

Despite Wil's advice to kick Vincent out of the apartment, Theo put up with him and supported him, a pattern that continued throughout Vincent's life. Fortunately, within a few months the situation improved, and Vincent, who always rose to the occasion when someone needed him, even offered to marry a troublesome woman with whom Theo had become involved.

Theo wrote home, "I have often asked myself if I have been wrong in helping him continually, and often have been on the point of leaving him to his own devices . . . but in this case I think I must continue in the same way. He is certainly an artist, and if what he makes now is not always beautiful, it will be of use to him later; then his work will perhaps be sublime."

As manager of the smaller Goupil's branch that exhibited nineteenth-century paintings, Theo sold mostly works by established artists. Only a few canvases by the Impressionists passed through his hands in the first year of Vincent's stay in

Paris. With his pale blond hair and melancholy face, the gentle, mild-mannered Theo wasn't adventurous, but he had a great eye for art. He managed to buy very cheaply the work of young artists he admired, and stacked the canvases in a storeroom above the shop. With Vincent's encouragement, Theo gradually came into his own as a dealer of new art. When Goupil mounted a show of works by Claude Monet, he sold ten landscapes, and later he sold some paintings by Paul Gauguin. Vincent, in his modest way, took no credit. He wrote to their sister Wil, "What I wanted to make you understand is this, that it is rather important that Theo has succeeded in inducing the business he manages to have a permanent exhibition of the Impressionists now." Yet Theo's debt to Vincent is clear. After his brother moved to Arles, Theo wrote to him, "You may do something for me if you like—that is go on as in the past, creating a circle of artists and friends for us, and which you have really more or less created since you came to France."

At thirty-five, Vincent realized that devoting his life to painting would require a personal sacrifice. Once he had hoped for a family; now he was losing the desire for marriage and blamed it on "this rotten painting." Theo, he said, should be the one to marry. That would please their mother as well as help preserve Theo's health.

By the end of his second year in Paris, Vincent had come to loathe the city he'd once so eagerly embraced. Always a man of extremes, he now saw disease and failure everywhere he turned. The art dealers were interested only in money, he thought, and he was sick of his fellow artists, with their petty fights and competition. "I will take myself somewhere down south, to get away from the sight of so many painters who disgust me as men," he told Theo.

Most of all he disgusted himself. Unhealthy from drink and lack of sleep, he longed for a calmer life in which to produce his art. He made up his mind to go south, "to look at nature from a brighter sky." Vincent, who theorized that a new art could be forged there, regaled Bernard with his grand scheme to start an artists' commune in the south of France.

He asked Bernard to come over to redo the apartment in such a way that Theo would feel less lonely when he was gone. They decorated the walls with fresh Japanese prints and set up an easel with one of Vincent's paintings. Bernard embraced his friend and promised to come to Arles to help build their colony of the future. Then, as a last nod to the Paris art world, Vincent and his brother visited the studio of the celebrated Pointillist painter Georges Seurat on their way to the train station. In Provence, Vincent fantasized, the weather would be warm, the countryside would look just like Japan, and his mental and physical health would improve. These hopes were short-lived, but he was about to achieve his dream of becoming a great artist.

Vincent in Arles

1888 – 89

I want to produce, to produce a lot and with a consuming drive.
—LETTER TO THEO, SEPTEMBER 1888

VINCENT'S FIRST VIEW of Arles was cold, deep snow. After a fifteen-hour train journey, he lugged his heavy baggage through the thick white drifts into the town, down an avenue of plane trees, through red stone towers, to the Hôtel Carrel, where he rented a room for five francs a night—too much money, in his opinion, and no warmth anywhere.

He came prepared for sunshine and friendly natives, but he had trouble settling in. His letters were full of complaints. The weather was terrible. Everything cost too much. He couldn't find decent food or good blue paint or correct information on the price of stamps. In addition, the townspeople, who spoke in their own peculiar dialect, didn't understand the Dutchman's French. "You have no idea of the slackness and the nonchalance of the people here," he wrote to Bernard. At first he agreed with the guidebooks that the women of Arles were beautiful, only to revise his opinion later. "They are, no question about it, really charming, but no longer what they must have been . . . for they are in their decadence." As for Arles, "It is a filthy town this, with old streets."

Arles had its roots in ancient times, with a still-standing Roman amphitheater and a magnificent medieval church. These were classic subjects for some artists, but Vincent thought of himself as modern, a man of his own time. Old buildings and ruins held no interest. Instead he painted a street scene of a butcher shop seen from a window, a landscape of the snowy fields, and a portrait of an old woman in the costume of the region.

The mistral, a seasonal wind that swept down the Rhône valley, made painting outside a struggle. Some claimed that a few days spent in the relentless sixty-mile-an-hour wind was an excuse for murder. To Vincent, the mistral was an unexpected handicap that "got on one's nerves badly." On days when he felt strong enough, he'd set up his canvas on an easel fastened into the ground with pegs. When the gales were too fierce for that, he laid the canvas flat on the ground and painted on his knees. Perhaps one of his first scenes, a snowy field painted in the short brushstrokes and light palette of the Impressionists, was done quickly because he was uncomfortable out in the cold. But he did describe the picture as "just like the winter landscapes that the Japanese have painted."

As Theo sent him money every month, Vincent felt obliged to let Theo know how hard he was working, writing long letters about his progress. "At present I feel pretty bad some days, but I don't worry about it in the least, as it is nothing but a reaction to last winter, which was out of the ordinary. . . . I must reach a point where my pictures will cover my expenses."

The letters chronicle the steps he took in organizing his compositions (possibly his way of defending his unconventional style) and also trace his mood swings. To Bernard, who was painting with Gauguin and other artists in Brittany, he wrote his most cheerful letters, to show how well he was doing. To Theo he tended to pour out his fears and insecurities. With the first signs of spring, his mood lightened and his letters became enthusiastic about his move to Arles and the abundance of subjects to paint. The wide plains and canals reminded him of Dutch scenery. He delighted in the women's multicolored clothes with yellow, green, and red stripes. Arles suddenly seemed as gay as Holland was gloomy.

In April, when the trees blossomed, he wrote to Bernard, "At the moment I am absorbed in the blooming fruit trees, pink peach trees, yellow-white pear trees. My brushstroke has no system at all. I hit the canvas with irregular touches of the brush, which I leave as they are. Patches of thickly laid on color, spots of canvas left uncovered, here and there portions that are left absolutely unfinished, repetitions, savageries; in short I'm inclined to think that the result is so disquieting and irritating as to be a godsend to those who have fixed preconceived notions about technique."

He described himself as being in "a frenzy of work," painting the pear and plum orchards laden with pink, white, and purple blossoms, trying to capture their fullness before they faded, and using up more than a hundred tubes of color. Then, worried that Theo couldn't afford to send him extra money to buy more, he did a dozen or more pen-and-ink drawings, mailing them off for his brother's approval.

Vincent had experimented briefly with a reed pen back in Nuenen. Now he found that the reeds, which grew in abundance in the marshes around Arles, were even better for his drawings. The reed pen allowed him to make the broad, flat strokes that imitated the fluid lines of Japanese artists. "Their work is simple as breathing, and they do a figure in a few sure strokes with the same ease as if it were as simple as buttoning your coat," he wrote. In his drawings of Arles, the jabs, dots, and hatching demonstrate a quick, flowing energy that would be characteristic of his style.

Not only was his painting unconventional, but in town Vincent himself was viewed an odd figure. In his old clothes and floppy hat, weighted down with all his equipment, wandering about at odd hours, especially at night, he didn't try to blend in with the local population. To paint outside in the dark, he rigged up a hat rimmed with candles and set up his easel on a street corner. Stars glimmered in the real sky and on the canvas. Flames flickered on his hat. "The night is more alive, more richly colored than the day," he said. This image of Vincent might seem romantic and amusing, but the townspeople of Arles were not used to artists. The adults saw him as bizarre, and the teenage boys jeered and made fun of him as he crept by, his head lowered and his back "loaded like a porcupine" with painting equipment.

The townspeople also viewed foreigners as legitimate targets for fleecing. Vincent regarded this custom fairly tolerantly, as one of the evils of a poor local economy—until his innkeeper tried to charge extra to store his canvases and then locked up his art supplies. Vincent took him to court and won, but he'd had enough of the inn and began hunting for a place of his own.

He soon found a space that suited him. "My house here is painted the yellow color of fresh butter on the outside with glaringly green shutters; it stands in the full sunlight in a square which has a green garden with plane trees, oleanders, and acacias. And it is completely whitewashed inside, and the floor is made of red tiles. And over it is the intensely blue sky. In this I can live and breathe, meditate, and paint." Unlike the dark, furniture-crammed houses of his relatives in Holland, the yellow house was simple, fresh, and carefully arranged by Vincent, from the white walls to the paintings he chose to hang. "This is a real artist's house," he said. The bathroom was in the building next door, but Vincent didn't view that as a big problem. He spent the money his brother sent him to furnish the two bedrooms with sturdy wooden beds, then followed it up with a letter asking for more, which, of course, softhearted Theo provided.

With his housing problems solved, Vincent felt upbeat. In his newly arranged studio at the yellow house, he had a place to paint when a raging mistral forced him inside. He continued his experiments with color, attempting to paint two still lifes of a table with a pot of flowers and other objects with "six different blues and four or five yellows and oranges." On sunny days he ventured out into the countryside to paint the fields and views of the town.

He was eager to find new subjects, so in early June he set off to see the Mediterranean for the first time. He traveled by a type of horse-drawn carriage called a diligence through the Camargue, where wild white horses roamed the countryside, to the fishing village of Stes.-Maries-de-la-Mer. There he found one of his most popular images. *Boats on the Beach* was completed in his studio in Arles, but his description of the preliminary study tells the story of a breakthrough in his work. He had noticed the brightly colored little boats, but as the fishermen put out to sea so early, he had time only to do a drawing. Proudly he sent it off to Theo, saying, "The Japanese draw quickly, very quickly like a lightning flash. . . . I have only been here a few months, but tell me this—could I, in Paris, have done the drawing of the boats in an hour?" Instead of using a tool to draw in perspective, he wrote, "this is done without measuring, just by letting my pen go."

Back in Arles in 1888, there was such a blazing sun that some of the farmers began their harvest early. Vincent, in a fever of creativity, painted canvas after canvas of the fields and crops around Arles. He would go out at daybreak and paint nonstop until sunset, striving for what he called "the high yellow note"—vivid color and emotion in perfect harmony. The color yellow had a special significance for Vincent. It stood for life and energy.

The drawing skills he'd labored for years to acquire in The Hague and Nuenen enabled him to paint with amazing speed—so quickly, in fact, that he justified it in a letter to Theo. "I must warn you that everyone will think that I work too fast. Don't you believe a word of it. . . . If the emotions are sometimes so strong that one works without knowing one works, then one must remember that it has not always been so, and that in time to come there will be hard days, empty of inspiration." Vincent feared he would run out of steam and suffer from painter's block.

But that was one problem he would never encounter. During one swelteringly hot week in June, Vincent produced ten paintings, and five drawings of the harvest. "Landscapes yellow—old gold—done quickly, quickly, quickly, in a hurry, just like the harvester, who is silent under the blazing sun, intent only upon his reaping." He constantly criticized and reevaluated the work, his quest for "the high yellow note" bringing its dissatisfactions along with its triumphs. Of the triumphs, his greatest one up to that point was the painting he called simply

Harvest at le Crau—a field of corn on the fertile plain called the Crau, painted in full sunshine from a hill.

The strain of these long, overwrought days affected his health. He wrote, "When I come home after a spell like that, I assure you my head is so tired that if that kind of work keeps recurring, as it has done since this harvest began, I become hopelessly absentminded and incapable of doing heaps of ordinary things." Then he confessed, "The only thing to bring ease and distraction is to sedate oneself by smoking heavily and drinking"—this despite his deteriorating health.

It was inevitable that he would crash, that he was headed for a complete breakdown, but he continued driving himself. With the same manic energy, he had pursued teaching, preaching, and missionary work without success; now he pursued painting. He had found what he was meant to do. "Left to myself, I rely on my intoxication with work . . . and then I let myself go without limits." He maintained that to be a real artist he had to push himself over the edge: "The more I am spent, ill, a broken pitcher, the more I become an artist, creator, in this revival of the arts." Yet when he was painting, he experienced a happiness that eluded him in the rest of his life. The paintings celebrated his elation. The artist, who had written earlier that his brushstrokes had no system, was producing works in a style that would forever be unique to him, even those canvases without his now-famous signature, the single name *Vincent*.

Arles: "A High Yellow Note"

1888 – 89

I would like to paint in such a way that everybody,
at least if they had eyes, would see it.

LETTER TO THEO, AUGUST 1888

IN HIS BRIGHT BLUE postman's uniform with gold buttons, Vincent's new friend, Joseph Roulin, sat stiffly posing for his portrait. Vincent thought the postman looked like Socrates, with his large head, ruddy cheeks, and long salt-and-pepper beard. He painted quickly, as Roulin could hardly contain himself. His wife had just delivered a baby girl, and he was "proud as a peacock and aglow with satisfaction." He promised Vincent he could paint the baby in her cradle, and then he proceeded to sing the "La Marseillaise," the French national anthem, in a terrible voice, vowing to christen his daughter at home instead of at church. Vincent thought him more interesting than anyone he'd met in Arles. When he finished the portrait, the Roulins invited him to stay for supper. Roulin, after a bottle of wine, expounded on his socialist politics and offered the younger artist advice about life. For Vincent, who long ago had lost faith in his own father, Roulin, "so wise and so trustful," became a father figure: "Roulin has a salient gravity and tenderness for me such as an old soldier might have for a young one." He painted eight versions of the postman, as well as portraits of Mrs. Roulin and their two sons. Despite his poverty, Roulin refused to be paid, so Vincent ended up buying him food and many drinks at the local café. He also gave the Roulins paintings. Spending time with them helped Vincent feel less lonely, more a part of a family life he missed.

Also at this time Vincent painted a flamboyant portrait of a soldier of the Algerian infantry, whom he gleefully described as "a man with a small face, a bull neck, and the eye of a tiger." The soldier faces the viewer in full Zouave uniform. His legs, clad in wild red pantaloons, are spread wide, taking up a fourth of the canvas. Vincent liked the style of this portrait—"vulgar, loud"—in opposition to the overly refined portraits that the rich commissioned in Paris. He painted his other friend in the regiment, Paul-Eugène Milliet, but complained that the young, handsome soldier was a bad poser and too much of a womanizer to sit still. Milliet probably wouldn't get the girls, Vincent grumbled to Theo, if he were an artist.

Though he often forgot mealtimes when he painted, Vincent was concerned about eating properly and wrote to Theo that he'd finally found a café that served decent food. Near his yellow house, the Café de la Gare was run by Mr. and Mrs. Ginoux. He painted her as a classically beautiful Arlésienne wearing an elegant black dress.

He also spent some nights living at a cheap inn, the Café Alcazar, before his yellow house was completed. The bar was open all night and attracted the "night prowlers," who had no money for lodging. Before long Vincent started on a painting of the interior, staying up for three nights and sleeping all day. He started it as a joke because, he said, he had paid the landlord so much money that he would "paint his whole rotten joint to repay himself." *The Night Café,* which he called "one of the ugliest I have done" because of the harsh contrasts of reds and greens, was explained in detail in a letter to Theo. Charming interiors painted by the Impressionists or the grand settings of the court painters held no interest for Vincent. "In my picture I have tried to express the idea that the café is a place where one can ruin oneself, go mad, commit crimes. In short I have tried to express the powers of darkness in a low public-housing, by using soft Louis XV green and emerald green, contrasting with yellow-greens and harsh blue-greens, and all this in an atmosphere of pale sulfur, like a devil's furnace."

A few painters passed through Arles, and one of them, the Belgian Eugène Boch, captured Vincent's imagination. They hiked, debated about art, and watched bullfights in the Roman amphitheater. In Boch he found the model he sought for a painting of a dreamer using exaggerated colors against a starry sky, with his face pale against the deep blue "like the mysterious brightness of a pale star in the infinite." The fanciful background of stars represented the character of an artist-poet to Vincent, who wrote, "I want to say something comforting, as music is comforting. I want to paint men and women with that something of the eternal." Seeking to infuse his portraits with a lasting quality, he was returning to sentiments he'd held in Holland before "I knew the Impressionists."

Boch, with his "face like a razor blade" and "very sensible ideas," according to Vincent, had plans to go to the Borinage to paint the coal miners. Vincent encouraged him, as he hoped Boch would start an artists' commune there. This could be a counterpart in the north to the one he dreamed of putting in place in his yellow house. It was criminal, he said, that young artists in Paris struggled so hard to survive, thus falling prey to a decadent life. In Arles, surrounded by natural beauty, he fantasized that artists would bond like brothers, sharing expenses, ideas, and eventually profits from the collective sale of their works. The group would forge a new direction in art, one that would surpass the spontaneous imagery of the Impressionists and convey a deeper feeling. This fantasy centered on the artist Paul Gauguin, whose work he admired above all his contemporaries. With Gauguin's help, he believed, his artists' colony could work, but first Vincent had to persuade him to move to Arles.

Vincent considered Gauguin a hero for his reckless but courageous decision to give up an affluent life to be an artist. As a teenager, Gauguin had run off to serve as a cabin boy on a ship. When he returned to Paris, he worked his way up as a stockbroker, enabling himself and his wife and their five children to live lavishly. In his spare time he studied painting, exhibiting a few pictures and winning critical praise. With typical bravado he quit his job to pursue art, and in less than three years he lost everything. His family left him and fled to his wife's native Denmark. Borrowing money from a friend, Gauguin moved from Paris to a village in Brittany, where his distinctive painting style slowly evolved.

But four years later Gauguin, now forty-four, ill and deeply in debt, wrote to Theo asking for help. Letters went back and forth from Paris to Arles to Brittany as Vincent lobbied Gauguin to join forces with him and persuade Theo to bankroll the artists' colony venture. Finally they struck a deal.

Gauguin would go to Arles, and Theo would send him 150 francs a month in exchange for paintings. Vincent was overjoyed at the thought of having a companion, someone who would make his life less lonely. In preparation for Gauguin's arrival, he decorated the house, hanging his best paintings in the guest room, including two dazzling still lifes of sunflowers painted as variations on the color yellow. They had to be painted quickly, "for the flowers fade so soon, and the thing is to do the whole in one rush." Vincent, extremely satisfied with these works, said, "If by the time I am forty I have done a figure piece as good as those flowers . . . I shall be the equal of any artist." He even suggested to Theo that it would be a good idea to make cheap prints of the sunflowers to brighten the rooms of working people.

His pride in the yellow house led him to spend his whole allowance fixing it up for his friend. He rushed to finish paintings, "living on twenty-three cups of coffee, with bread that I still have to pay for." He had gas lines run downstairs to light the main room so that they could work in the evenings. Frantic to impress Gauguin, he had "no time to think or feel; I just go on painting like a steam engine."

To give Theo some idea of the interior, Vincent painted a picture of his bedroom. Unlike the garish *Night Café*, *Vincent's Bedroom at Arles* offers a lighter mood with softer, more soothing colors. "Color is to do everything . . . and is to be suggestive here of rest or of sleep in general. In a word, looking at the picture ought to rest the brain, or rather the imagination." To achieve this sense of calm, he used paler complementary colors—walls of blue violet, a butter yellow chair and bed, a scarlet coverlet, sheets and pillows of yellowish green, an orange washstand, and a blue washbasin. He painted no shadows and no stippling, as the picture was meant to be in the flat tints of Japanese prints. This remained one of his favorite paintings, and he copied it three times, with one copy intended for his mother, one for Theo to sell, and the other to save. In his letters he continued to remind Theo that his best work must be kept intact.

In the fall Gauguin sent his trunk ahead to Arles and soon arrived himself by the night train. He first went to the café, where the landlord recognized him from the self-portrait he had sent to Vincent. If Vincent presumed that his friend would be overwhelmed by the yellow house and especially by his paintings, he was in for a big disappointment. Gauguin said almost nothing about either, except to write years later that what struck him was how messy the house looked. "Between two such beings as he and I, the one a perfect volcano, the other boiling inwardly too, a sort of struggle was preparing. In the first place, everywhere and in everything I found a disorder that shocked me. His color box could never contain all those tubes, crowded together and never closed." Most likely Gauguin was shocked by the power and skill of Vincent's new work. He hadn't expected such competition.

At first the two artists enjoyed each other's company. To Vincent's delight, Gauguin took over the cooking and the household accounts, as he was more organized. They worked side by side in the vineyard, in the public garden, and in the fields, facing in opposite directions, painting one great canvas after another. At night in the cafés they discussed art over dinner and many drinks.

Gauguin encouraged Vincent to paint from his imagination instead of from life. Vincent wrote, "Gauguin has more or less proved to me that it is time I was varying my work a little. I am beginning to compose from memory." Vincent's passion at the time was robust, heightened color; Gauguin's was imagining his subjects from memory. Although both men believed that the artist's role was to move beyond imitating nature to a deeper construction of reality, their styles and techniques differed. Vincent favored thick paint and vigorous brushstrokes. Gauguin used thin, flat planes of strong color and simplified shapes, giving his painting a dreamlike quality.

Vincent could take advice from the older artist on his work, but he remained his obstinate self. "Our arguments are terribly electric, sometimes we come out of them with our heads as exhausted as a used electric battery." By December Gauguin pronounced Arles a filthy dump and its inhabitants ugly. Vincent wrote, "I think myself that Gauguin was a little out of sorts with the good town of Arles, the little yellow house, where we work, and especially with me." The truth was that Gauguin had never been enthralled with the idea of an artists' commune. He'd needed some immediate financial support and saw Arles as a stopping-off point before he sailed for Tahiti. Vincent had put his hopes on a man who was basically self-absorbed and out for himself.

The two paintings Vincent did of his own wooden chair and Gauguin's fancier armchair, the seats empty except for objects symbolic of the artists' very different personalities, represent Vincent's sadness at the situation. The chairs also work as portraits of the two artists. Gauguin is represented by a candlestick, two modern French novels, and a richly textured carpet to indicate his vitality and sophistication. Vincent's more modest chair holds his pipe and tobacco. Onions sprouting from a wooden box emphasize his affinity with the simpler, rural life. But if Vincent intended the paintings to convince Gauguin to stay, they made no difference. Gauguin had

informed Theo of his imminent departure. Vincent's yearning to have a companionable housemate as well as "a colorists'
school in the south" was merely a pipe dream. Gauguin
lapsed into stony silence, and no matter how hard Vincent
tried to please him, the older artist remained surly and
uncommunicative.

Nerves on edge, Vincent began to act strangely. Gauguin
wrote, "During the latter days of my stay, Vincent would become excessively rough and noisy, and then silent. On several
nights I surprised him in the act of getting up and coming over
to my bed. . . . It was enough for me to say quite sternly,
'What's the matter with you?' for him to go back to bed without a word and fall into a heavy sleep."

Another time Vincent crept in, laughing madly, and wrote
on the walls, "I am the Holy Spirit; my spirit is whole." Gauguin went on to claim that Vincent had attacked him in a bar
by throwing a glass of absinthe at his head and then had
passed out. The next morning Vincent told Gauguin he had
only a vague memory of what had happened.

On Christmas Eve, at dinner, Vincent and Gauguin probably drank too much wine and started arguing. Gauguin might
have goaded Vincent about his inability to paint from memory or his lack of success with women. When he threatened
again to leave Arles, Vincent became agitated and unruly.
Gauguin took off alone to get some fresh air. As he headed
across the Place Victor Hugo, he recognized Vincent's quick,
short steps behind him. Vincent, reported Gauguin, looked
quite mad and approached him in the street saying, "You are
taciturn, I shall be likewise." Gauguin gave him a piercing
glare, and Vincent lowered his head and ran off toward home.

Alarmed, Gauguin checked into a small hotel nearby and

went to bed. Vincent returned to the yellow house and slashed off his earlobe with a razor. After he stopped the bleeding, he stuck a large beret on his head and brought the severed ear, wrapped in newspaper, to a brothel that he and Gauguin frequented. Calling for a girl named Rachel, he handed this gory Christmas gift to her, saying, "Keep this object like a treasure." Back at the house, he passed out in his bed and lay there unconscious until the police, who had heard about the incident, found him the next day.

Gauguin showed up around noon to find a crowd gathered outside in the street. He entered, stared at Vincent, lifeless and rolled in his sheets, and told the police, "Awaken this man with great care, and if he asks for me, tell him I left for Paris. The sight of me may prove fatal for him." Gauguin actually returned to Paris a few days later with Theo, who had taken a train down to Arles to be with his brother. The two artists never saw each other again.

Vincent couldn't or wouldn't remember the details of this terrible night, but one thing is true: In a deranged or drunken moment, he forever marked his place in history as the mad artist who cut off his ear.

Within two weeks Vincent was discharged from the hospital. "I am completely recovered and am at work again and everything is normal," he wrote to his mother and his sister Wil in Holland. And to his credit, he went back to the brothel and apologized to Rachel for the outrageous act he couldn't remember. She assured him that half the people in town were crazy and told him not to worry.

Back at the yellow house, he painted yet another self-portrait—a forlorn, resigned figure standing in his studio, a Japanese print in the background. With the familiar fur cap covering the top of his bandaged ear, Vincent stares out into space. "What happened?" he seems to ask. He painted several still lifes to prove to himself he could still work, and then turned to a painting he had begun before he was hospitalized, a portrait of Roulin's wife. He titled it *La Berceuse* (woman rocking a cradle) because she holds in her hands a rope for rocking an unseen cradle. He and Gauguin had read a book about the hard lives of Icelandic fishermen, and Vincent planned the painting as a response, so that the sailors in their fishing boats "would feel the old sense of being rocked come over them and remember their own lullabies." The motherly, consoling figure was comforting to Vincent as he recovered from his illness. He wrote to Theo that in his mind's eye he had visited every room in their childhood home, and had seen the views, the church, the kitchen garden, even the magpie's nest in a tall acacia in the graveyard. "Whether I really sang a lullaby in colors is something I leave to the critics." He painted five versions of this portrait. After he let his model choose one, he gave a copy to Gauguin in trade, two to Theo to sell, and the other to Theo to keep.

Vincent reassured Theo that work and sensible living would cure him, but in spite of all his efforts, he was readmitted to the hospital within a month. This time he imagined that people were trying to poison him, that he heard voices. His cleaning woman, bewildered by his strange behavior—withdrawals into silence, alternating with wild outbursts—informed the police. Again he rallied, this time after ten days.

The villagers of Arles were not sympathetic, and his few friends were helpless to protect him. Bands of teenagers, whom he called "hooligans," followed him in the streets and threw rocks at his house. "Crazy redhead," they taunted, climbing up and peering in his windows as he crouched inside. Gossips swore he went around town shouting and grabbing women about their waists. The neighbors signed a petition claiming he was dangerous. They feared for their safety.

Busy in Paris, Theo was unable to come to his brother's rescue. His bosses at Goupil were unlikely to give him extra time off. More significant, just before Vincent's first attack, Theo had become engaged to Johanna (Jo) Bonger from Amsterdam, who was the sister of their good friend Andreis Bonger. Vincent realized that Theo's attention would be taken up by his new wife, but he wished him well.

"I assure you that I am much calmer since I picture that you have a companion for good. Above all, do not imagine that I am unhappy." Once Vincent had counted upon leading a normal life with a wife and children, but at this point he knew it would never happen. Vincent implored Theo to do nothing, as he was "in full possession of my faculties and not a madman. . . . Let things be without meddling."

The police locked him in a cell with a guard at the door. Shut in a small room with one window, he spent his days feeling helpless, like a caged animal. He tried to be patient, realizing that to rant and rave against the injustice would only build a case against him. "What a staggering blow between the eyes it was to find so many people here cowardly enough to join together against one man, and that man ill," wrote Vincent, who always felt such compassion toward people in distress.

Paul Signac, a painter friend from Paris, was traveling to the south of France, and Theo asked him to look in on Vincent. Signac thought Vincent seemed fine, and he persuaded the authorities to let Vincent go out for a few hours so that they could visit the yellow house. The police had sealed the house, but Signac smashed the lock and forced it open. There, immersed in the shadows, were Vincent's paintings of sunflowers, landscapes, portraits, all created in the year since Signac had last seen him.

Many years later, the impressed artist wrote to another friend, "Imagine the splendor of those white washed walls, in which flowered those colorings in their full freshness. Throughout the day he spoke to me of painting, literature, socialism. In the evening, he was a little tired. There had been a terrific spell of mistral and that may have enervated him. He wanted to drink about a quart of essence of turpentine from the bottle that was standing there. It was high time to return to the asylum."

Yet right after their visit, Signac wrote to Theo, telling him he had found Vincent in perfect health and sanity and quoting Vincent's doctor as suggesting that his patient needed only a tranquil place to work to avoid another attack. "How dismal the life he is living must be for him," said the sympathetic Signac.

A month later Vincent was discharged from the hospital. Vincent's landlord, under pressure to find a new tenant, evicted him from the yellow house. With nowhere to live, Vincent's only option was to pack up his paintings, store some at Ginoux's inn, and ship the rest off to Theo in Paris, letting go forever of his dream of an artists' colony.

The doctor diagnosed Vincent's problem as seizures triggered by mental stress and poor physical condition. Three other doctors over a two-month period indicated that he was seriously ill. "M. Rey [Vincent's doctor] says that instead of eating enough and at regular times, I kept myself going on coffee and alcohol. I admit all that, but at the same time it is true that to achieve the high yellow note I attained last summer, I had to be pretty well keyed up." In his 444 days in Arles, he had produced two hundred paintings and more than a hundred drawings and watercolors. His compulsive behavior had enabled him to make extraordinary paintings, but it also had taken a toll on his health.

St.-Rémy: The Asylum
1889–90

The days you least anticipate you find a subject which holds its own with the work of those who have gone before us.

LETTER TO THEO, MID-NOVEMBER 1889

EVICTED FROM HIS yellow house and anxious about his health, Vincent turned to his friends for advice. The postman Roulin, who had visited him every day in the hospital, couldn't help. He'd been transferred to a new district and would be leaving town. Dr. Rey offered Vincent a small apartment in his house, but Vincent worried about his ability to live alone. As a last resort, a local Protestant minister named Salles, whom Theo had enlisted to check on Vincent, suggested he consider a mental institution in the town of St.-Rémy, about fifteen miles away. Vincent decided to apply for admission with the understanding that he be allowed to paint. Theo assured him it was just for a rest, that he would soon recover.

There have been many differing theories about Vincent's condition, and much has been written about it. The director of the hospital in St.-Rémy wrote on his admission form that in his opinion Vincent suffered from "acute mania, with hallucinations of sight and hearing which have caused him to mutilate himself by cutting off his ear. . . . My opinion is that Monsieur van Gogh is subject to epileptic fits at very infrequent intervals."

Was he a lunatic? A dangerous madman? If so, how could he have painted such extraordinary masterpieces, especially during his stay in the asylum? The most popular theory, generally accepted, is that he suffered from an unusual form of epilepsy, possibly complicated by the effects of absinthe or digitalis poisoning. Today there is medication for epilepsy, but then none existed, and those who suffered from it found no relief. Certainly there were moments when Vincent lost his reason, but he was not insane. Other than the weeks when he was incapacitated from an attack, he painted masterpieces and wrote intelligent, thoughtful letters about them. Between attacks he sometimes lacked energy and felt weak and nervous, but his creative ability was not affected.

Completely lucid when he arrived at the asylum, Vincent described his surroundings in precise detail. Originally a monastery in medieval times, St.-Paul-de-Mausole, as it was called, stood at the edge of a charming little village surrounded by olive groves and tall cypress trees, two miles from the craggy limestone hills called the Alpilles. "I have never been so peaceful as here and in the Hospital in Arles—to be able to paint a little at last. Quite near here there are some little mountains, gray and blue, and at their foot some very green cornfields and pines. I shall count myself very happy if I can manage to work enough to earn my living. For it worries

me a lot when I think I have done so many pictures and drawings without ever selling one."

From his small cell with its faded green flowered curtains, he
looked through the bars on his window and watched the sun
rising on a square field of wheat. He painted scenes from that
window but never included the bars. With only ten male patients, there were thirty empty rooms in the dormitory, so he
received permission to use one of them as a studio. He tried to
adapt to his constricted new life. "The food," he wrote, "tastes
rather moldy, like a cockroach-infested restaurant in Paris. . . .
As these poor souls do absolutely nothing (not a book, nothing
to distract them but a game of bowls and a game of checkers),
they stuff themselves with chick peas, beans, and lentils." This,
he joked, caused a few digestive problems.

He ventured from his cell to paint in the courtyard, bordered by an overgrown garden. A profusion of irises had
caught his eye. He set up his easel near the fountain to paint
masses of purple petals glowing against the emerald foliage
and azure sky. The other patients watched him from a respect-
ful distance. Later, as he moved through the long, arched hall-
ways of the hospital, he heard their cries. Sensitive to human
suffering, Vincent tried to comfort the other inmates, often
staying with them when they had attacks. He listened to the
descriptions of their symptoms, amazed that they, too, heard
voices and saw distorted shapes.

"I think I have done well to come here; first of all, by seeing
the reality of the life of the various lunatics and madmen in
this menagerie, I am losing the vague dread, the fear of the
thing. And little by little I can come to look upon madness as
a disease like any other." He was able to see the effects of
epilepsy on several of the patients, which helped him understand his own condition. Optimistic by nature, Vincent chose

to make the best of the situation, to benefit from the regularity of his life there. But sometimes the pitiful behavior of the patients depressed him. They shouted constantly, tore off their clothes, and smashed furniture. Other than soaking in a tub of cold water for two hours twice a week, they received no treatment for their illness. It upset him that Dr. Peyron, the director of the asylum, had so little motivation to improve the situation.

After a month he talked Peyron into allowing him to go out into the surrounding fields to paint. An attendant went along with him. With new oils and canvas sent by Theo, Vincent immersed himself in the beauty of the countryside. "Since it is just the season when there is an abundance of flowers and thus the color effects," he wrote to Theo, "it might be wise to send me another five meters of canvas." He muted the violent colors of the previous summer as a way of seeking a calmer mood for himself. Drawn to the tall cypress trees, he said, "They have not been done the way I see them."

Road with Cypress and Star, with its dynamic shapes and thick application of paint, shows Vincent at the height of his powers. It is his most dramatic painting of a subject that dominated his attention in St.-Rémy. Here he reached his goal to paint a "modern" landscape by representing the spirit of a place, rather than simply picturing a tree. The somber form of the tree is like a portrait—a lonely giant against a brooding landscape. Perhaps the lone tree spiraling into an agitated sky matched the state of his own mind.

By mid-July he had completed an astonishing number of artworks: thirty-one paintings and forty drawings. "What is a drawing?" he asked. "It is working oneself through an invisible iron wall that seems to stand between what one feels and what one can do." Drawn with a reed pen, his sketches of cypress trees are masterful, filled with pulsating spirals, short curvy strokes, and contrasting light and dark lines. Patterns of dots and overlapping curlicues give the drawings the rich effect that color achieves in painting. His works in St.-Rémy incorporated these qualities, producing a sense of movement and energy.

He felt he might be cured, even though Dr. Peyron told him he would need to stay there at least a year. But he had reason to feel optimistic, as he was able to work all day. He spent his evenings reading in English the historical plays of William Shakespeare, sent by Theo.

Then one day he opened a letter from Theo and read that Theo and Jo were expecting a baby. Nothing in Vincent's letters supports the notion that he was jealous. Perhaps he worried about Theo's financial support. But a few weeks later, after an upsetting visit to Arles to retrieve some of his paintings, he suffered a severe seizure. He began hallucinating and tried to swallow his paints. Quickly his attendant restrained him. Afterward Vincent couldn't remember what had happened. But he did write, "When you suffer much . . . the very voices seem to come from afar. During the attacks I experience this to such a degree that all the persons I see then, even if I recognize them . . . seem to come toward me out of a great distance, and to be quite different from what they are in reality."

He avoided working outside again for two months and refused to leave his bedroom. His mind might have been clear, but he felt weak and demoralized. When he started drawing again, the nuns who worked at the asylum would not return his paints. They realized Vincent was an artist, but he was hardly famous, and his works were strange enough to be dismissed.

As someone brought up in the austere Dutch Reformed Church, Vincent found the faith of the nuns superstitious and stifling. It so disturbed him that he began to experience frightening religious hallucinations. Yet after each attack he rallied, forcing himself to "eat like two now, work hard, and limit my relations with the other patients for fear of a relapse. I am now trying to recover like a man who meant to commit suicide, and finding the water too cold, tries to regain the bank."

Away from his friends and family in an alien place, he became homesick, and thoughts of his childhood and the landscape of Brabant, the family garden, the little graveyard, and the church haunted him. He made a number of drawings from memory. The looming cypress in *The Starry Night* can be found in the south of France, but the tall church steeple in the small village nestled at the foot of the mountains is Dutch. From memory and from life, he combined these two settings purposefully to create a lasting impression, not simply a pretty scene. Looking at the stars swirling in the night sky produces a dizzying effect, as if the artist were painting an ecstatic vision. Although this painting departed from reality, it was no hallucination. In this carefully worked-out composition, the vigorous lines were inspired by German woodcuts. It symbolized for Vincent a deeply spiritual mood. *The Starry Night* is bolder and more visionary than the night paintings done in Arles. There he concentrated on color; in St.-Rémy line became the insistent element. When he sent the painting to Theo, his brother didn't comment on the sky but only on the familiar landscape.

Jo gave birth to a son, naming him Vincent Willem after his uncle, and Theo asked Vincent to be the godfather. Vincent didn't feel up to traveling, but he painted a beautiful canvas of almond branches against a blue sky for the new baby, as if the child lying in the cradle were looking up through flowering arms.

Almost as soon as he'd finished the canvas, he had another attack and was "down like a brute . . . Difficult to understand things like that," he said, "but alas." Practically overnight he recovered and was back at his easel. Purple irises, olive orchards, and later the mountains occupied him as well as a few portraits, including Mrs. Roulin (from memory) and Trabuc, the asylum's head attendant. Theo sent him prints by Daumier and Millet to copy. Millet's painting *The Sower*, with its theme of peasant life, inspired more than twenty works. Vincent wrote, "I am trying to do something to console myself, for my own pleasure."

Just as the Sower paintings symbolized a life-giving force, his paintings of the Reaper stood for death. "I see in this reaper—a vague figure fighting like the devil in the midst of the heat to get to the end of his task—I see in him the image of death, in the sense that humanity might be the wheat he is reaping. . . . But there's nothing sad in this death, it goes its way in broad daylight with a sun flooding everything with a light of pure gold."

Like many artists or writers who have felt exiled from their own countries, Vincent was highly sensitive to his surroundings. In St.-Rémy his paintings of the cypress trees, the olive groves, and the mountains were meant to express the essence of the south, offering "at best a sort of whole, 'Impressions of Provence.' " During his year in the asylum, between some debilitating attacks, he averaged two paintings a week, along with detailed descriptions in letters to Theo about his progress.

In the winter of 1890 a brilliant young critic, G. Albert Aurier, saw Vincent's paintings at Père Tanguy's shop and at Theo's apartment in Paris. Dazzled by Vincent's powerful style, Aurier wrote a glowing article about him in an avant-garde magazine, *Mercure de France,* calling him "a terrible maddened genius, often sublime, sometimes grotesque." This was the first published article written about Vincent, who, instead of rejoicing, wrote Theo, "Please ask M. Aurier not to write any more articles on my painting . . . it pains me more than he knows." But it wasn't being called "maddened" that upset him. Vincent thought Aurier had been too flattering and that others, such as Gauguin, deserved more praise.

Because of Aurier's article, six of Vincent's paintings were sent to an exhibition in Brussels. There *The Red Vineyard* was purchased for 400 francs. Even though Vincent traded paintings and sold a few drawings during his lifetime, *The Red Vineyard* is often referred to as the only real sale he ever made. His friend Toulouse-Lautrec, as well as Renoir and Cézanne, had paintings in the exhibition. When a Belgian artist called Vincent's pictures the work of an ignoramus, Toulouse-Lautrec challenged him to a duel, but the French contingent stepped in to stop him.

Almost immediately after the sale, Vincent suffered a relapse. "As soon as I heard that my work was having some success, and read the article," he wrote to his mother, "I feared at once I should be punished for it. . . . Success is the worst thing that can happen in a painter's life." This reaction to praise echoes his behavior as a little boy when he tore up a drawing his mother admired.

Spring arrived, marking a year since he had admitted himself to the asylum. Now he obsessed about leaving. "I must make a change, even a desperate one." He knew he couldn't risk living alone, so letters went back and forth between him and Theo about his various options. Gauguin, who was living in Brittany, politely refused to offer him a room, telling friends later, "Not that man! He tried to kill me!" Perhaps, Vincent wrote Theo, he could stay with the painter Camille Pissarro, who had been so kind to him in Paris. But Pissarro's wife, the tougher of the couple, said she was afraid to have him around her children.

The fatherly Pissarro came up with a solution. He knew of a small town about twenty miles from Paris called Auvers-sur-Oise where a physician named Dr. Gachet resided. This doctor, he said, was sympathetic to artists and knew a little about psychiatry. So it was decided that Vincent would go north again. This move proved to be his last.

Auvers-sur-Oise: The Last Refuge

1890

Well, the truth is, we can only make our pictures speak.
—LAST LETTER TO THEO, JULY 1890

ON HIS WAY to Auvers, Vincent stopped in Paris to meet Theo's wife, Jo, and his new nephew for the first time. Jo presumed Vincent would be frail and was surprised to see "the sturdy, broad shouldered man, with healthy color, a smile on his face, and a very resolute appearance." In fact, she thought Vincent looked healthier than her husband.

Theo brought Vincent into the room where his namesake lay sleeping in a cradle. The two brothers, who had been through so much, stood side by side looking down at young Vincent with tears in their eyes. Then Vincent turned to Jo and pointed to the crocheted coverlet. "Do not cover him up with too much lace, little sister," he said.

Jo wrote that the three-day visit was a happy occasion, but Vincent's letters afterward tell a different story, focusing on some unresolved issues. Nothing had been settled about his allowance. And seeing his paintings stored in the "bedbug infested hole" at Père Tanguy's upset him. On some of his canvases the swirling paint was half an inch thick, and stacking them in Tanguy's small spare room caused the paint to stick and crack. "By keeping them in good condition, there would be a greater chance of getting some profit out of them," Vincent wrote.

From Theo's letters to Vincent, it is clear that he believed strongly in his brother's talent, but he was careful, almost reticent, about showing the work outside his apartment. There was no way Vincent would have exhibited at Goupil, Theo's gallery. After all, its stuffy director had once fired him. In addition, Theo, who was committed to the Impressionists, did not fully appreciate Vincent's generation of painters. Their raw colors and bold imagery put him off. Vincent, concerned about the sale of his paintings, told his brother not to compromise if he didn't feel the work was ready. Yet with practically every batch of canvases that Vincent sent to Paris he included a note about their commercial prospects, indicating how aware he was of the business of art.

Unsure of his finances, Vincent arrived in Auvers in late spring, settling into a little room on the third floor of an inn owned by the Ravoux family. Vincent described Auvers as "very beautiful, having among other things a lot of old thatched roofs. . . . It is real country, characteristic and picturesque." The first day he set off down the long slope dotted with cottages to the Oise River to draw. The sky was filled with crows circling the wheat fields, and the pink-and-white almond trees were in bloom. Looking around, Vincent could understand why Auvers had attracted other artists, such as Cézanne and Pissarro.

Paul-Ferdinand Gachet, the physician recommended by his friend Pissarro, lived with his teenage son and daughter in a large villa "full of old things, black, black, black except for some impressionist paintings . . . a strange little fellow," wrote Vincent. In his sixties with a mane of thick red hair and a long, sad face, Gachet fancied himself an artist and made etchings on his own press. Vincent's first impression was that the doctor seemed as distraught as his patients. Gachet invited Vincent for dinner and, much to his relief, offered to treat the fidgety artist if he should feel ill or depressed. Vincent complained that Gachet served too much rich food but found himself enjoying their conversation about art and literature. Over brandy Gachet invited him to paint in his home. This appealed to Vincent, who started the next day on a portrait of the doctor, in whose face he saw "the heartbroken expression of our time."

This would be a modern portrait, said Vincent, one that didn't glorify the sitter as traditional portraits did. "I should like to paint portraits which would appear after a century to the people living then as apparitions. So I do not endeavor to achieve this by photographic resemblance, but by means of our impassioned expressions, using our knowledge of and our modern taste for color as a means of arriving at the expression and intensification of character. So the portrait of Dr. Gachet shows you a face the color of an overheated brick, and scorched by the sun."

His deep blue suit and the lighter blue sky emphasize the doctor's pale face as he leans on his elbow at an angle, his expression melancholy. The yellow novels on the table represent the doctor's intellectual side, and the purple flower of a foxglove, a medicinal herb used to treat disorders of the nerves, indicates his profession.

Vincent said that he and the doctor were very much alike; Vincent not only related to Gachet's suffering and vulnerability but also had grown fond of him.

Vincent quickly discovered other subjects in Auvers. With his shoulder bent slightly toward his wounded ear, he set off to paint each day just as the sun rose, returning late in the afternoon to the inn. The Ravoux family, who called him Monsieur Vincent, found him quiet and polite, with a gentle manner. After his evening meals, he played with their two-year-old daughter, drawing pictures of the sandman on a slate before she went off to bed. He also made a portrait of the family's thirteen-year-old daughter, Adeline. He painted it in one sitting, smoking his pipe, not saying a word until he finished. Although the Ravouxes were not very enthusiastic about the painting, Vincent gave it to them. In 1988 one of the two portraits Vincent did of Adeline was sold at auction for $13.5 million.

As his room was too small to use as a studio, Vincent mainly painted landscapes outdoors. He produced a remarkable amount of work, some seventy to eighty studies, during his stay in Auvers. A Dutch painter, Anton Hirschig, who also lived at the inn, recalled that Vincent piled his finished canvases casually in the corner of a hut where the goats were usually kept. No one seemed interested in looking at them. Vincent talked to Hirschig of his plans to exhibit the work in Paris and the possibility of taking a trip with Gauguin. Considering the fact that Gauguin had abandoned him in Arles after that terrible night, the idea was a credit to Vincent's good heart and his spirit of forgiveness.

In June Theo and Jo brought the baby to Auvers for a picnic. Vincent met them at the train station with a bird's nest for the baby and insisted on carrying his nephew around to show him all the animals at Dr. Gachet's: eight cats; eight dogs; numerous chickens, rabbits, and ducks; and even a peacock. When the loud crowing of a rooster frightened the baby, Vincent laughed, shouting, "The cock crows cocorico." They had lunch outside and afterward took a long walk. "The day was so peacefully quiet, so happy that nobody would have suspected how tragically our happiness was to be destroyed for always a few weeks later," wrote Jo. Vincent, elated by the visit, hoped they would see more of each other now that he lived so close to Paris. Yet there were some warnings in letters to Theo about Vincent's mounting despair. In one he wrote of his little nephew, "I should like him to have a soul less unquiet than mine, which is foundering."

What happened in Auvers that sent Vincent on a downward spiral after weeks of productive work? He had been able to dedicate himself to painting without worrying because of Theo's support. Monthly and sometimes weekly checks arrived, along with extra art supplies whenever Vincent needed them. But in June a letter from Theo announced some disturbing news. The baby had fallen seriously ill, and Theo believed the illness was a reaction to the milk in Paris, which he described as poisonous. Jo, he wrote, was exhausted from the baby's crying, and he was beside himself with worry. He went on to tell Vincent that he was angry with his employers, whom he referred to as "those rats," and was thinking of resigning. He mentioned he was short of money. Vincent responded to Theo's letter by urging him to come to Auvers, where country life would be healthier for his family.

When the baby's health had improved a little, Vincent insisted on going to Paris to visit Jo and Theo. He found the couple in the midst of marital problems, Jo exhausted from caring for a sick baby and climbing up and down the stairs to their fourth-floor apartment. His conversations with them were tense, and visits from friends left him jumpy. Quickly he returned to Auvers and wrote them a note:

> My impression is that since we were all rather stupefied and perhaps a little overwrought, it matters little to any very clear definition of the position we are in. You rather surprise me by seeming to wish to force the situation while there are disagreements between you. Can I do anything about it— perhaps not—but have I done anything wrong, can I do anything that you would like me to do?

Jo tried to reassure Vincent that things would be all right, and Vincent replied:

> It is no slight thing when we feel our daily bread is in danger; no slight thing when for other reasons we feel that our existence is fragile. Back here I also felt very sad and continued to feel the storm which threatens you to be weighing on me. I try to be fairly cheerful, but my life is threatened at the very root. . . . Being a burden to you, you felt me to be rather a thing to be dreaded.

This last line goes to the root of Vincent's worry, his sense of causing a hardship to Theo and his family. It also is likely that Theo told Vincent about his own health problems. In letters Vincent often expressed concern about Theo's chronic cough and other signs of his delicate condition. Vincent's anxiety grew worse, and he lost confidence in his own doctor. "I think we must not count on Dr. Gachet at all. First of all he is sicker than I am, I think, or just as much. Now when one blind man leads another blind man, don't they both fall into a ditch?"

Several days after returning from Paris, Vincent showed up at Dr. Gachet's house and flew into a rage for no good reason. A painting he admired of a woman lying on a couch with a Japanese fan had not been framed. In a loud voice he accused the kindly doctor of gross neglect. His abrupt manner frightened Dr. Gachet's children, who wrote later that they stood "rooted to the spot." After a stern look from the doctor, Vincent turned, leaving the house without another word.

He threw himself into his work, "though the brush almost slipped from my fingers." Writing to reassure his mother that he was "in a mood of calmness," he described his efforts to capture the delicate blue and violet skies and the immense wheat field against the hills.

Wheatfield with Crows, a dark and somber painting, indicates that his mood was far from calm. In this brooding work, one of his last paintings, there are turbulent skies, crows flying wildly toward the viewer, and a field of overripe wheat bisected by a road seeming to lead nowhere. A dirt path in the foreground curves off the sides of the canvas. The horizon seems to roll forward, as if the world is closing in with no escape. The artist, who in his darkest moments had created optimistic paintings celebrating life, had lost hope.

In his last letter, possibly a draft of one he'd sent to Theo earlier, he began, "There are a lot of things I might write you about but to begin with the desire to do so has so much left me, and I feel the uselessness of it." He went on to tell Theo how important his part had been in his painting: "Through me you have your part in the actual production of some canvases that will retain their calm even in the catastrophe. . . . Well, my own work, I am risking my life for it and my reason has half foundered because of it . . . but what's the use?" Perhaps knowing the letter sounded too much like a goodbye note, he stuffed it in his smock, where it was found a few days later.

On the morning of Sunday, July 27, almost ten years to the day since he had begun his artistic journey in the Borinage, Vincent set out for the wheat fields with his easel. At some point he took out a revolver (supposedly purchased to frighten crows), put the gun to his stomach, and shot himself. This was not a moment of insanity or a seizure; it was an act of considered despair. Like the reaper of his paintings, he faced death in the wheat fields under the burning sun.

It was dusk when Vincent returned to the inn. The Ravoux family, sitting on the terrace of the café after the busy Sunday meal, noticed he was bent over, stumbling. Mrs. Ravoux asked, "Monsieur Vincent, we worried, we are glad to see you come home. Has anything unfortunate happened to you?"

"No, but I . . . ," said Vincent without finishing the sentence.

Mr. Ravoux followed him upstairs and found him in bed with his face to the wall. Vincent showed him his wound, saying softly, "I wanted to kill myself."

Gossip about Vincent's attempted suicide spread around town, and the next morning the police arrived and demanded to see for themselves. There were French laws against suicide.

"You know you don't have the right to do so?" one told the dying man.

Vincent said in his quiet voice, "This body is mine and I am free to do with it what I want."

When Dr. Gachet heard the news, he quickly sent Hirschig to Paris with a letter for Theo that began, "With greatest regret, I must bring you bad tidings." Rushing to Auvers, Theo found Vincent with Dr. Gachet and another physician from the village. Vincent lay in bed smoking his pipe, saying nothing until Theo knelt down near him. As Vincent was conscious, Theo assumed his brother would pull through, but it was not to be. Vincent van Gogh died of infection from the unremoved bullet on July 29, 1890. His last words were "I wished I could pass away like this."

Emile Bernard traveled from Paris for the funeral of his friend. He wrote, "On the walls of the room where the body lay, all his last canvases were nailed, forming a sort of halo around him, and rendering his death all the more painful to the artists who were present by the splendor of the genius which radiated from them." His coffin, placed on the billiard table at the inn, was covered with white linen and strewn with yellow sunflowers and dahlias. Yellow was the color he had chosen to express his deepest emotions—"the high yellow note." His brushes and easel were placed in front of the coffin.

Vincent was buried in Auvers, in the little cemetery behind a stately Gothic church he had painted. Artists, family, and friends gathered for the funeral. In his eulogy on the hill of the cemetery, with the blue sky and the wheat fields beyond, Dr. Gachet said through his tears, "He was an honest man and a great artist. He had only two goals, humanity and art."

Theo, broken with grief, wrote this poignant letter to his mother after Vincent's funeral: "One cannot write how grieved one is nor find any comfort. It is a grief that will last and which I certainly will never forget as long as I live; the only thing one might say is that he himself has the rest he was longing for. . . . Life was such a burden to him; but now, as often happens, everyone is in praise of his talents. . . . Oh Mother, he was my own, own brother."

Postscript

SHORTLY AFTER VINCENT'S DEATH, Theo moved to a larger apartment in his building so that he could mount a memorial show of his brother's paintings. But within six months, Theo's mental and physical health deteriorated to such a degree that his wife, Jo, brought him back to Holland, where, riddled with a progressive, chronic disease, he died in a clinic. Theo was buried beside his brother in the little cemetery in Auvers-sur-Oise.

Jo's brother suggested she throw the paintings out and get on with her life. The other members of the van Gogh family had no interest or faith in Vincent's art. But Jo refused to abandon the work that had meant so much to her husband and his brother. Through her determined efforts the paintings and drawings, as well as the letters, survived. She organized exhibitions and wrote a biography of her soon-to-be-celebrated brother-in-law. Painstakingly she catalogued more than 680 letters and arranged to have them published. Within ten years the success that had eluded him in life came

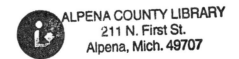

posthumously, with exhibitions of his work, critical praise, and buyers from all over Europe and the United States clamoring for his paintings.

A hundred years after his death, *Still Life with Sunflowers*, painted in Arles, sold at auction for $29.9 million. The poster of Vincent's sunflowers is one of the most popular reproductions in the world, thus making Vincent's wish come true that it might "brighten the rooms of working people." *Portrait of Dr. Paul Gachet*, painted in Auvers a few short months before his suicide, was auctioned for a record-beating $82.5 million. His story has been the subject of a Hollywood movie, a bestselling novel, and countless art books. Would Vincent have been pleased? It's hard to know what the reaction of such a complicated man might have been, but one thing is certain: He had foreseen that after his death his paintings would find an admiring audience.

Fate did not grant Vincent a wife, children, good health, wealth, or charm. But he was given another gift—the ability to see deeply into nature, to put on canvas his own ardent soul. His feeling for the rhythms of life, his sympathy for his fellow man, his yearning for love, and his understanding that what mattered was not worldly success but spirituality and a passion for work all poured into his painting. On this work he would be judged and found great. His legacy to us is not only powerful, vibrant paintings but also articulate, poetic letters. Through these we can relive his story, the story of Vincent, the consummate artist.

Biographical Time Line

1853	On March 30 Vincent Willem van Gogh is born in Groot-Zundert, a town in the southern Netherlands.
1857	Theodorus van Gogh (Theo) is born.
1869	Vincent apprentices at Goupil et Cie, art dealers in The Hague.
1875	Vincent is transferred to Goupil's branch in Paris. The Reverend Theodorus van Gogh is transferred to a small congregation in Etten.
1876	Vincent is dismissed from Goupil and travels to England, where he works as a teacher in Ramsgate and Isleworth.
1877	Vincent returns to the Netherlands and works in a bookstore in Dordrecht for four months. To prepare for the ministry, he moves to Amsterdam.
1878	Vincent goes to Brussels to take a course for evangelists. He volunteers for a mission in the Borinage, a coal mining district in Belgium.
1881	Vincent moves back into his parents' home in Etten and falls in love with his widowed cousin Kee Vos-Stricker.

1882	The Reverend Theodorus van Gogh moves to another parsonage in Nuenen. Vincent moves to The Hague to study art.
1882–83	Vincent lives in The Hague with Sien Hoornik and her children.
1883	Vincent works in Drenthe for four months.
1883–85	Vincent lives in his parents' home and then by himself in his studio in Nuenen.
1884	Vincent has an ill-fated romance with Margo Begemann.
1885	Vincent's father dies suddenly. Vincent moves to Antwerp to study art.
1886	Vincent attends the Antwerp Academy of Fine Art for two months and then moves to Paris to live with Theo.
1886–88	Vincent works at Corman's studio for several months. He meets many young artists in Paris, such as Emile Bernard and Paul Signac.
1888	Vincent moves to Arles, a town in the south of France, in February. Paul Gauguin comes to live with him in October. Theo becomes engaged to Johanna (Jo) Bonger. Vincent cuts off his earlobe and is sent to a hospital in Arles.
1889	Theo and Jo are married in April. Vincent admits himself to an insane asylum in St.-Rémy in May.
1890	Jo and Theo become parents of a son, Vincent Willem, in January. In May Vincent moves to Auvers-sur-Oise, not far from Paris. On July 27 Vincent shoots himself, and he dies on July 29, at the age of thirty-seven. In September Theo mounts a memorial exhibition of his brother's work in their apartment in Paris. Theo becomes both mentally and physically ill, and Jo takes him to a clinic in Holland.
1891	Theo dies at the age of thirty-four in a clinic in Holland.

Museum Locations

Some museums where you will find paintings by Vincent van Gogh:

Rijksmuseum Vincent van Gogh, Amsterdam, the Netherlands
  The works from the estate of the van Gogh family are preserved
  here, having been kept for many years by Theo van Gogh's
  widow, Mrs. J. van Gogh-Bonger, and her son, Dr. Vincent W.
  van Gogh. Despite the fact that she had to keep a boardinghouse
  to support herself and her young son when she returned to Holland after her husband's death, Jo van Gogh-Bonger devoted her
  life to keeping Vincent's legacy alive. This group of letters,
  Japanese prints collected by the artist, his drawings, and his
  paintings is the largest collection of his works and is administered
  by the Vincent van Gogh Foundation.
Rijksmuseum Kroller-Muller, Otterlo, the Netherlands
  This once private collection, now open to the public amid acres
  of gardens and woods, includes some of van Gogh's greatest
  works.

Boston Museum of Fine Arts
Chicago Art Institute
Cleveland Museum of Art
Fogg Museum, Cambridge, Massachusetts

Metropolitan Museum of Art, New York
Museum of Fine Arts, Houston
Museum of Modern Art, New York
National Gallery, Washington, D.C.
Norton Simon Art Foundation, Los Angeles
Philadelphia Museum of Art
Saint Louis Art Museum

Glossary of Artists and Terms

EMILE BERNARD (1868–1941): A poet as well as a painter, Bernard was a prodigy on the Parisian scene at age eighteen. He painted with both Gauguin and Vincent, but he is now best known for having written a book about Vincent.

PAUL CÉZANNE (1839–1906): A painter who also worked in the south of France (in Aix-en-Provence). Vincent claimed that some of his shaky forms must be a result of painting in the mistral. Like Vincent, Cézanne wanted to penetrate beyond the reality of nature, but to Cézanne what lay beyond were the abstract forms of the cylinder, the sphere, and the cone.

EDGAR DEGAS (1834–1917): Degas refused to paint outdoors, as the other Impressionists did, claiming that "art is not a sport." His sharply cropped pictures, original use of space, and paintings of contemporary subject matter—ballet dancers and horse racing—made him one of the Impressionists even though he broke with them over color.

CHARLES DICKENS (1812–70): An English novelist who wrote many famous books, including *A Christmas Carol, Oliver Twist,* and *A Tale of Two Cities,* that dealt with the suffering of the poor and the social injustices of his era. Vincent, who had great sympathy for the poor, found Dickens's themes important and his stories moving.

FLEMISH: A term used to describe the people, language, and styles of northern Belgium.

FRANC: A French monetary unit.

PAUL GAUGUIN (1848–1903): A painter who was the central figure of a movement called Symbolism, which explored the spiritual nature of art. Gauguin's flat planes of color outlined in black were influenced by stained glass and folk art. He was a flamboyant figure who went to Brittany to live among the peasants and later to Tahiti to paint the natives, whose simplicity and faith he tried to capture in his paintings.

GUILDER: A Dutch monetary unit.

THE HAGUE: The capital of the province of South Holland.

HAGUE SCHOOL (1860–1900): A group of artists, including Anton Mauve, who painted Dutch landscapes in an idealized style with a strong sense of the light of this northern region.

FRANS HALS (1581?–1666): A great seventeenth-century portrait painter from Antwerp. Vincent spent hours studying his works in the museum in Amsterdam.

IMPRESSIONISM: A movement originated in France in the 1850s by a group of artists who were interested in exploring the scientific effects of light and movement and in representing impressions of the moment in their paintings. They celebrated the everyday pleasures of middle-class life, especially through scenes of leisure activities.

EDOUARD MANET (1832–83): A French artist who was more interested in the structure of painting than its expressive content. His followers were called Impressionists, but he disliked the term.

ANTON MAUVE (1838–88): Vincent's cousin, a Dutch painter of landscapes and still lifes, who briefly taught Vincent.

JEAN-FRANÇOIS MILLET (1814–75): A French painter who lived in the village of Barbizon near Paris. His lovingly painted scenes of peasant life influenced Vincent's art, and Vincent made many copies of Millet's paintings, both to learn and to "console" himself.

CLAUDE MONET (1840–1926): Impressionism took its name from one of Monet's paintings—*Impression: Sunrise*. He dedicated his life to painting his immediate visual observations of light and color in nature, working in the open air. Early in his career he had to beg his friends for money to buy bread for his children, but eventually his paintings of water lilies, haystacks, gardens, and other sun-drenched scenes gained him a wide following.

CAMILLE PISSARRO (1830–1903): A painter who was the white-bearded father figure to many young artists, helping, among others, Vincent, Cézanne, and Gauguin. Pissarro's son Lucien, also a painter, was a friend of Vincent's in Paris.

POST-IMPRESSIONISTS: A term later used by critics to identify Vincent van Gogh and the other artists of his generation who were trying to go beyond the Impressionists to put emotion back into their painting through strong color, shape, or line.

REMBRANDT VAN RIJN (1606–69): The greatest genius of Dutch art in the seventeenth century, whose use of light and expressive content Vincent admired. He is the only artist who painted more self-portraits than Vincent.

PIERRE-AUGUSTE RENOIR (1841–1919): Renoir's happy disposition is evident in his paintings, both the early Impressionist works, in which the subject matter often was people having a good time, and his later round and rosy nudes, painted in a more classical style.

GEORGES SEURAT (1859–91): Seurat finished only seven paintings in ten years, canvases that brilliantly demonstrate Pointillism, which used dots of color to produce an optical effect on the canvas.

PAUL SIGNAC (1863–1935): A Pointillist, like his friend and mentor Georges Seurat.

HENRI DE TOULOUSE-LAUTREC (1864–1901): Toulouse-Lautrec painted Parisian nightlife with a satirical and unsentimental eye, from the viewpoint of what he self-mockingly called "elbow height" in reference to his own short stature.

JAN VERMEER (1632–75): A Dutch painter of everyday life in the seventeenth century, known for his magical use of light. His serene mosaics of colored surfaces have a distinctly modern quality.

Notes

The four published versions of the letters of Vincent van Gogh we consulted are listed in the bibliography. However, in these notes we keyed all the letters to *The Complete Letters of Vincent van Gogh*, published by Little, Brown in 1958.

CL = Complete Letters, vol. 1, vol. 2, vol. 3. *All letters are from Vincent to Theo unless otherwise noted.*

V and T = *Vincent and Theo van Gogh: A Dual Biography* by Jan Hulsker.

VGSP = *Van Gogh—A Self-Portrait*, selected by W. H. Auden.

TL = *The World of van Gogh, 1835–1890* by Robert Wallace.

VGMM = *Van Gogh* by Melissa McQuillan.

VVGRM = *Vincent van Gogh* by Evert van Uitert et al.

VGSRA = *Van Gogh in St.-Rémy and Auvers* by Ronald Pickvance.

Prologue

Pages 1 to 3. Most of the thoughts and descriptive phrases in the prologue are taken from Vincent's letters to Theo. Whole days outside with a little bread: CL, vol. 2, Letter 509, p. 610; Plains as beautiful and infinite as the sea: CL, vol. 2, Letter 509, p. 610;

Everywhere now there is old gold, bronze, copper: CL, vol. 2, Letter 497, p. 583; Emerald green, Prussian blue, crimson lake: CL, vol. 2, Letter 475, p. 543; The labor of balancing six essential colors: CL, vol. 2, Letter 507, p. 606; Like an actor on the stage in a difficult part: CL, vol. 2, Letter 507, p. 606; Spanish flies, gold and green: CL, vol. 2, Letter 506, p. 602; Grasshoppers sing loud as a frog: CL, vol. 2, Letter 502; Eaten by mosquitoes: Letter 509, CL, vol. 2, p. 609.

A Brabant Boy, 1853–75

Pages 5 to 6. Replacement child theory: Albert J. Lubin, psychologist (*Stranger on the Earth*, 1972) builds a strong case, using circumstantial evidence and contemporary psychological theories, that Vincent's problems were caused by his position in the van Gogh family as a replacement for his dead brother.

Pages 6 to 7. Rosebush story and destroyed drawing story: Johanna van Gogh-Bonger, who talked to Vincent's mother, tells both of these stories in her short biography of Vincent, published as a foreword to *The Complete Letters*. Memoir, CL, vol. 1, p. xxi.

Pages 7 to 8. Mr. Provily's school: Vincent referred at least twice in his letters to this painful parting with his parents, at greatest length in Letter 82a. CL, vol. 1, p. 78.

Page 8. Vincent's education: The information about Vincent's schooling is from Jan Hulsker. V and T, pp. 11–12.

Page 10. Vincent writes to thank Theo for his visit in Letter 1. CL, vol. 1, p. 1.

Page 10. Everybody liked dealing with Vincent: Mr. Tersteeg's letter to the parents is quoted by Johanna van Gogh-Bonger. Memoir, CL, vol. 1, p. xxiv.

Page 11. Love for Eugénie Loyer. Johanna van Gogh-Bonger reports that the van Gogh family believed that Vincent's behavior changed when Eugénie refused to marry him. Memoir, CL, vol. 1, pp. xxiv–xxv.

Page 13. *When the apple is ripe:* Vincent first wrote to his brother about the firing in Letter 50. CL, vol. 1, p. 45.

Vincent in England, 1876–77

Page 15. *No one of us will ever forget the view:* Letter 67, CL, vol. 1, p. 57.

Page 16. *The ground we walk on:* Letter 63, CL, vol. 1, p. 55.

Page 16. *No professions in the world:* Letter 70, CL, vol. 1, p. 61.

Page 17. *If their son wanted to be an evangelist:* Jan Hulsker quoted this from an unpublished letter written by Mr. van Gogh to his son Theo. V and T, p. 37.

Page 17. *Sorrow is better than joy:* Vincent's sermon is published in full in *The Complete Letters.* CL, vol. 1, pp. 87–91.

Pages 17 to 18. Vincent's life at the bookstore: In 1890, in response to a newspaper article, Mr. P. C. Gorlitz, Vincent's roommate while he was working at the bookstore, wrote a letter about his friend for publication. The story about Vincent's diet, churchgoing habits, and religious texts comes from Gorlitz. VGSP, p. 37.

Pages 17 to 18. The grandson of the owner of the bookstore also was interviewed and told his father's story of Vincent's work habits. Document 94a, CL, vol. 1, p. 108.

Pages 18 to 19. Vincent's worries about school: He wrote to Theo about his anxieties in Letters 98 through 119. CL, vol. 1, pp. 119–163.

Page 19. Remedy for suicide: Letter 106, CL, vol. 1, p. 135.

Page 19. Vincent's appearance: Mendes da Costa wrote an article about his experience tutoring Vincent that included a description of Vincent's appearance, his habits, and his reason for leaving his studies. Document 122a, CL, vol. 1, p. 170–171.

Page 20. *Oh, sir, I really don't care:* In 1912, more than twenty years after Vincent's death, when his accomplishments as a painter had been recognized, a memoir published in a Brussels newspaper gave an account of Vincent in school there. Document 126a, CL, vol. 1, p. 181.

The Missionary, 1879–80

Page 21. Visit to the Marcasse: Vincent wrote a spectacular letter to his brother Theo on his trip down the mine. The descriptive phrases in the first two paragraphs are taken from that letter. Letter 129, CL, vol. 1, p. 186.

Page 22. *The baker's wife saw him:* M. Louis Piérard collected and published memories of Vincent in the Borinage, including the baker's account of his mother's meeting with Vincent. VGSP, p. 64.

Page 23. Vincent's response to advice from the family: Theo came to visit, bringing good advice from the family, and Vincent wrote to him about it. Letter 132, CL, vol. 1, p. 191.

Pages 24. Vincent's trip to Courrières: Vincent was not corresponding with Theo when he walked to Courrières, but a few months later when they were back in touch, he wrote to Theo about the trip, making a humorous story out of his arduous journey. Letter 136, CL, vol. 1, p. 204.

Pages 25 to 26. *Such a man* and *I always think the best way to know God:* Vincent wrote a long, rambling, and tremendously moving letter to Theo about the difficult lessons learned in what he referred to as his molting time. Letter 133, CL, vol. 1, pp. 193–200.

Page 26. *Send me what you can:* Letter 134, CL, vol. 1, p. 200.

Pages 26 to 27. Bread and chestnuts: Letter 138, CL, vol. 1, p. 211.

In Love, 1881–83

Page 30. *Queer little fellow:* The descriptions of Vincent's person and behavior at this time come from interviews with local people of the Brabant who knew him then. In the 1920s Mr. Benno J. Stokvis traveled around the countryside talking to those who remembered the pastor's odd son. Document 165b, CL, vol. 1, p. 290.

Page 31. Vincent confronts the Strickers: Vincent wrote Theo a dramatic and bitterly humorous account of his attempt to see Kee. Letter 164, CL, vol. 1, p. 283.

Page 31. Vincent puts his hand in the lamp: Vincent did not tell his brother this part of the scene with Uncle Stricker until a few months later. Letter 193, CL, vol. 1, p. 351.

Page 32. Vincent leaves the parsonage: Vincent's account to Theo of the quarrel with his father extends over several letters, but in letter 169 Vincent wrote on Theo's letter his answer to Theo's accusation that he had behaved badly, so we have both sides of the correspondence. Letter 169, CL, vol. 1, p. 298.

Page 33. Vincent's account of lessons with Mauve. Letters 170–172, CL, vol. 1, pp. 303–310.

Page 33. *You are no artist:* Vincent sometimes included dialogue in his letters. In this one he repeats many of Mr. Tersteeg's insults. Letter 179, CL, vol. 1, p. 320.

Page 33. Time you earned your bread: Letter 181, CL, vol. 1, p. 323.

Page 34. *You have a vicious character:* Letter 192, CL, vol. 1, p. 349.

Page 35. *Am I free to marry:* Letter 193, CL, vol. 1, p. 352.

Page 35. Parents' threat to put him in a madhouse: Letter 216, CL, vol. 1, p. 411.

Page 36. *Who am I in most people's eyes:* Letter 218, CL, vol. 1, p. 416.

Page 36. *I see that nature has told me:* Letter 228, CL, vol. 1, p. 448.

Page 37. Expectation of a short life: Letter 309 (postscript), CL, vol. 2, p. 105.

Page 37. *She has never seen what is good:* Letter 317, CL, vol. 2, p. 123.

Vincent the Dog, 1883–85

Page 40. *I feel what Father and Mother:* Letter 346, CL, vol. 2, p. 231.

Page 40. *With real courage:* Letter from Mr. van Gogh to Theo, V and T, p. 171.

Page 42. The story of Margo Begemann: Vincent was a great reader most of his life. He believed that if he hadn't been a painter, he might have been a realistic novelist. In letters like these, he demonstrates his storytelling ability. Letters 377 and 378, CL, vol. 2, pp. 305–310.

Page 43. *I scoff at your technique:* One of his pupils in Nuenen, Van de Wakker, talked about Vincent's unusual painting technique. V and T, p. 188.

Page 43. Description of Vincent's studio: Another of Vincent's students was Anton Kerssemaker, a prosperous tanner, who had taken up painting in middle age. He published an amusing account of his days with Vincent. The description comes from him. Document 435c, CL, vol. 2, pp. 443–449.

Page 43. *This morning I talked things over with Vincent:* Johanna van Gogh-Bonger quoted from Mr. van Gogh's last letter to Theo. Memoir, CL, vol. 1, p. xxxviii.

Page 44. *Those people eating* and *If a peasant picture smells of bacon:* Letter 404, CL, vol. 2, p. 370.

Page 45. Vincent on Impressionists: Letter 402, CL, vol. 2, p. 366.

Page 46. Vincent in Antwerp: The fellow pupil at the academy in Antwerp, Mr. Victor Hageman, later recalled the impression Vincent made. Document 458a, CL, vol. 2, p. 507.

Page 47. *In a time of financial crisis:* Letter 454, CL, vol. 2, p. 497.

A Country Bumpkin in Paris, 1886–87

Page 49. Vincent's note to Theo: VGMM, p. 44.

Pages 50–51. Description of the brothers' apartment: Johanna van Gogh-Bonger must have heard about it from Theo and her brother, who often was a guest there. Memoir, CL, vol. 1, p. xl.

Page 51. *You would not recognize Vincent:* Theo wrote a reassuring letter to their worried mother. V and T, p. 226.

Page 52. Vincent in Corman's studio: V and T, p. 232.

Page 53. Account of Vincent's hissing through his teeth: Hulsker quoted one of Vincent's fellow students, A. S. Hartrick, who wrote his memoirs, including memories of Vincent, in 1939. V and T, p. 231.

Vincent and Friends, 1887–88

Page 56. Suzanne Valadon's story of Vincent at Toulouse-Lautrec's studio told to Florent Fels: TL, p. 53.

Page 57. Tanguy's sale of a painting: TL, p. 51.

Page 59. *It is as if he had two persons:* V and T, p. 246.

Page 60. *What I wanted to make you understand:* Vincent wrote this letter to his youngest sister, Wilhelmien. Letter W4, vol. 3, p. 431.

Page 60. *You may do something for me:* Relatively few letters survive from Theo's side of the correspondence. This is from one of them. Letter T3, CL, vol. 3, p. 533.

Page 60. *I will take myself somewhere down south:* Letter 462, CL, vol. 2, p. 521.

Vincent in Arles, 1888–89

Page 63. *You have no idea of the slackness:* Letter B7, CL, vol. 3, p. 495.

Page 64. The women of Arles: Letter 482, CL, vol. 2, p. 558.

Page 64. *At present I feel pretty bad:* Letter 474, CL, vol. 2, p. 541.

Page 65. *At the moment I am absorbed:* Letter B3, CL, vol. 3, p. 478.

Page 66. *My house here is painted the yellow color:* Letter W7, CL, vol. 3, p. 443.

Pages 67 to 68. *The Japanese draw quickly:* Letter 500, CL, vol. 2, p. 590.

Page 68. *I must warn you that everyone will think that I work too fast:* Letter 504, CL, vol. 2, p. 598.

Page 68. *Landscapes yellow—old gold—done quickly:* Vincent often wrote to his fellow artist and friend Bernard about artistic concerns. Letter B9, CL, vol. 3, p. 499.

Page 69. *When I come home after a spell:* Letter 507, CL, vol. 2, p. 606.

Page 69. *The more I am spent, ill, a broken pitcher:* Letter 514, CL, vol. 2, p. 620.

Page 69. Happiness in his work: Letter 507, CL, vol. 2, p. 607.

Arles: "A High Yellow Note," 1888–89

Page 71. *Proud as a peacock:* Vincent often wrote about Roulin, this time in a letter to Wil. Letter W5, CL, vol. 3, p. 439.

Page 72. *Such as an old soldier:* Letter 583, CL, vol. 3, p. 148.

Page 72. *A man with a small face:* Letter 501, CL, vol. 2, p. 591.

Page 73. *In my picture I have tried to express:* Letter 534, CL vol. 3, p. 31.

Page 73. *I want to say something comforting, as music is comforting:* Letter 531, CL, vol. 3, p. 25.

Page 75. *If by the time I am forty:* Letter 563, CL, vol. 3, p. 108.

Page 75. *Living on twenty-three cups of coffee:* Letter 546, CL, vol. 3, p. 67.

Page 75. *Color is to do everything:* Vincent was very aware of the psychological effects of color, as this letter shows. Letter 554, CL, vol. 3, p. 86.

Page 76. Paul Gauguin's description of the yellow house: Gauguin gave himself a big pat on the back for his contributions to his friend Vincent's work in the account *Avant and Après*, published fifteen years after Vincent's death, V and T, p. 312.

Page 77. *Our arguments are . . . electric:* Letter 564, CL, vol. 3, p. 109.

Page 77. *I think myself that Gauguin was a little out of sorts:* Letter 565, CL, vol. 3, p. 110.

Page 79. The story of the ear: There are two versions of what happened on December 23. Dr. Hulsker believes that the first story Gauguin told their mutual friend Bernard about Vincent's terrible accident is more likely the truth than the version Gauguin recounted fifteen years later in his book *Avant and Après*. The first is the one we have followed. In the second, more melodramatic version of the story, Gauguin claimed that Vincent threatened him with a razor, something he didn't mention at the time. V and T, pp. 322–323.

Page 79. *Awaken this man with great care:* This quote also came from Gauguin's account in *Avant and Après*. V and T, p. 323.

Page 79. *I am completely recovered:* Vincent wrote this letter to his mother and his youngest sister, Wil, who lived with her. Letter 569a, CL, vol. 3, p. 114.

Page 80. Memories of the garden in Groot-Zundert: Letter 573, CL, vol. 3, p. 128.

Page 80. *A lullaby in colors:* Vincent wrote this letter to a fellow Dutch artist, A. H. Koning. Letter 571, CL, vol. 3, p. 123.

Page 81. *I assure you that I am much calmer:* Letter 573, CL, vol. 3, p. 126.

Page 81. *In full possession of my faculties* and *What a staggering blow between the eyes:* Vincent describes his unjust imprisonment and asks Theo not to meddle. Letter 579, CL, vol. 3, p. 139.

Pages 81 to 82. Description of Signac's visit: Letter 581, CL, vol. 3, p. 145.

Page 82. Signac's account of his visit: Document 590b, CL, vol. 3, p. 166.

Page 82. *How dismal the life:* Signac wrote to Theo, and also to Vincent, inviting him to come to nearby Cassis to paint. Vincent did not go. Letter 581a, CL, vol. 3, p. 145.

St.-Rémy: The Asylum, 1889–90

Page 86. Doctor's admission notes on Vincent: V and T, p. 352.

Page 86. *I have never been so peaceful as here:* Vincent wrote this letter to his brother Theo's new wife, Johanna, whom he addressed as Dear Sister. Letter 591, CL, vol. 3, p. 169.

Page 87. *The food tastes rather moldy:* Letter 592, CL, vol. 3, p. 173.

Page 87. *I think I have done well to come here:* Letter 591, CL, vol. 3, p. 169.

Page 88. *Since it is just the season when there is an abundance of flowers:* This letter is an example of one of the many Vincent wrote to Theo asking for more art supplies or money. Letter 593, CL, vol. 3, p. 179.

Page 90. *Eat like two:* Letter 605, CL, vol. 3, p. 212.

Page 91. *I see in this reaper:* Letter 604, CL, vol. 3, p. 202.

Page 92. Vincent is upset by Aurier's review: Vincent wrote several more letters on the subject but in the end was grateful for the praise. Letter 626, CL, vol. 3, p. 253.

Page 92. *As soon as I heard that my work was having some success:* Vincent wrote this letter to his mother and his sister Wil. Letter 629a, CL, vol. 3, p. 262.

Auvers-sur-Oise: The Last Refuge, 1890

Page 95. *The sturdy, broad shouldered man* and *do not cover him up with too much lace:* Memoir, CL, vol. 1, p. 1.

Page 96. *Bedbug infested hole:* Letter 648, CL, vol. 3, p. 293.

Page 96. Description of Auvers: Letter 635, CL, vol. 3, p. 273.

Page 97. Description of Dr. Gachet's house: Letter 635, CL, vol. 3, p. 273.

Page 97. Dr. Gachet's character: Letter 638, CL, vol. 3, p. 276.

Page 97. *I should like to paint portraits:* Vincent. wrote this letter to Wil. Letter W22, CL, vol. 3, p. 469.

Page 98. Vincent at the Ravoux family's inn and Adeline Ravoux portrait: Adeline Ravoux wrote about Vincent's relationship with her family and the artist painting her portrait years after his death, in 1956. V and T, pp. 423 and 428.

Page 99. *The day was so peacefully* . . . : Memoirs, CL, vol. 1, p. lii.

Page 100. *My impression is that since we were all rather stupefied:* Letter 647, CL, vol. 3, p. 293.

Page 100. *It is no slight thing:* Letter 649, CL, vol. 3, p. 495.

Pages 100 to 101. *I think we must not count on Dr. Gachet:* Letter 648, CL, vol. 3, p. 294.

Page 101. Account of the episode over the painting with Dr. Gachet recounted in 1956 by Paul Gachet, his son, who indicated that his father thought Vincent might have had a gun in his pocket, but Paul Gachet later retracted the story. V and T, pp. 442–443.

Pages 101 to 102. Last letter found in Vincent's pocket: Letter 652, CL, vol. 3, p. 298.

Page 102. Vincent returns wounded to the inn: This account is part of the memoir written by Adeline Ravoux in 1956. V and T, p. 444.

Page 103. Vincent's funeral: Vincent's friend Bernard described the funeral in a letter to the critic Aurier. VGSRA, p. 219.

Page 103. *Oh Mother, he was:* Johanna van Gogh-Bonger quoted Theo's letter to his mother in her memoir. CL, vol. 1, p. liii.

Bibliography

Bonafoux, Pascal. *Van Gogh: The Passionate Eye*. Translated by Anthony Zielonka. New York: Harry N. Abrams, 1992.

Cabanne, Pierre. *Van Gogh*. London: Thames and Hudson, 1963.

Dorn, Roland, and Keyes, George S. et al. *Van Gogh Face to Face: The Portraits*. New York: Detroit Institute of Arts/Thames and Hudson, 2000.

Erickson, Kathleen Powers. *At Eternity's Gate: The Spiritual Vision of Vincent van Gogh*. Grand Rapids, Mich.: William B. Eerdmans, 1998.

Hammacher, A. M., and Renilde Hammacher. *Van Gogh*. London: Thames and Hudson, 1982.

Heinich, Nathalie. *The Glory of Van Gogh: An Anthropology of Admiration*. Translated by Paul Leduc Browne. Princeton: Princeton University Press, 1996.

Homburg, Cornelia et al. *Vincent van Gogh and the Painters of the Petit Boulevard*. New York: Saint Louis Art Museum/Rizzoli International, 2001.

Hulsker, Jan. *Vincent and Theo Van Gogh: A Dual Biography*. Ann Arbor: Fuller Publications, 1990.

Lubin, Albert J. *Stranger on the Earth: A Psychological Biography of Vincent van Gogh*. New York: Henry Holt/Da Capo Press, 1996.

McQuillan, Melissa. *Van Gogh*. New York: Thames and Hudson, 1989.

Nemeczek, Alfred. *Van Gogh in Arles*. New York: Prestel, 1995.

Pickvance, Ronald. *Van Gogh in Arles*. New York: Metropolitan Museum of Art/Harry Abrams, 1984.

——————. *Van Gogh in St.-Rémy and Auvers*. New York: Metropolitan Museum of Art/Harry N. Abrams, 1986.

Saltzman, Cynthia. *Portrait of Dr. Gachet: The Story of a Van Gogh Masterpiece*. New York: Viking, 1998.

Schapiro, Meyer. *Van Gogh*. New York: Harry N. Abrams, 1983.

Stone, Irving, ed. *Dear Theo: The Autobiography of Vincent van Gogh*. New York: Plume, 1995.

Uitert, Evert van, et al. *Vincent Van Gogh*. 2 vols. New York: Rizzoli, 1990.

Wallace, Robert. *The World of Van Gogh, 1853–1890*. New York: Time-Life Books, 1969.

Editions of Letters

Van Gogh: A Self-Portrait. Selected by W. H. Auden. New York: Thames and Hudson, 1961.

The Letters of Vincent van Gogh. Selected and edited by Ronald de Leeuw, translated by Arnold Pomerans. New York: Penguin, 1996.

The Letters of Vincent van Gogh. Edited and introduced by Mark Roskill. New York: Touchstone/Simon and Schuster, 1997.

The Complete Letters of Vincent van Gogh. 3 vols. Boston: Little, Brown, 1958.

Photography Credits

Index

About the Authors

Jan Greenberg and Sandra Jordan are the authors of several acclaimed books about art, including *Frank O. Gehry: Outside In* and *Chuck Close Up Close*, as well as three companion books, *The Painter's Eye*, *The Sculptor's Eye*, and *The American Eye*. Greenberg, the author of many noteworthy books for young readers as well as a teacher and an art educator, lives in St. Louis. Jordan, an editor and a photographer as well as a writer, lives in New York.

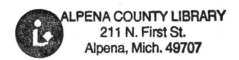